MW01264847

IT Management - 101

Fundamentals to <u>Achieve More</u>

Mike Sisco

Copyright © 2002 by Michael L. Sisco

More titles by Mike Sisco available at www.mde.net/cio

ISBN 0-7414-1191-1

Published by:

PUBLISHING.COM

519 West Lancaster Avenue
Haverford, PA 19041-1413
Info@buybooksontheweb.com
www.buybooksontheweb.com
Toll-free (877) BUY BOOK
Local Phone (610) 520-2500
Fax (610) 519-0261

Printed in the United States of America
Printed on Recycled Paper
Published June, 2002

Introduction

The challenge of managing technology resources has never been more demanding than it is today. Change occurs more rapidly in companies today and technical people are in more demand than ever before, especially good people.

People and companies respond to positive leadership. Strong leadership skills give a technical manager an edge in creating and maintaining a stable business environment, one that will accomplish much more than the norm and help the company achieve excellent results.

In this publication, I take an approach that will apply to any level of IT manager. Whether you are an accomplished Chief Information Officer (CIO) or a technical resource aspiring to become an IT manager, the material will be helpful.

The material contained in **IT Management-101** has been developed from my experience of managing technical organizations of all sizes for more than 20 years. The examples included are 'real life' examples of approacxhes I've seen that work, or that did not work. The tools have been incorporated or developed by me to assist in managing technical resources.

The bottom line: "Everything contained within this publication and my other publications in the **IT Manager Development Series** has been part of how I've managed IT organizations for many years".

Two tools are used to enhance the material or to clarify a point within this publication:

Sidebar: *an example or additional information provided to clarify a point.*

Personal Note: *a personal experience or "war story" used to reinforce the point being made.*

Managing organizations at a high level is serious business, but having fun along the way is half the battle. I hope you find the material helpful in your quest and I welcome your feedback. You may contact me at *mike@mde.net* .

The **IT Manager Development Series** includes the following titles:

> IT Management-101
> Developing an IT Business Plan
> Building a Successful IT Organization
> Building a Strategic IT Plan
> IT Project Management
> IT Staff Motivation and Development
> IT Asset Management
> What to Look For in a CIO
> Acquisition - IT Due Diligence
> Acquisition - IT Assimilations

All the tools plus many more are packaged in MDE's **IT Manager ToolKit.** The ToolKit includes 80 tools that I have developed and used over the past 25 years of managing IT organizations.

To learn more about the Series or the ToolKit, log onto *www.mde.net/cio.*

Mike Sisco

About the Author

Mike Sisco has been a senior IT manager and CIO for more than 20 years. From his earliest data processing days in the Marine Corps and at IBM, Mike has always been a high achiever. In the Marine Corps, he was assigned full operations management responsibility of a 24x7 data processing unit normally assigned to Marines of three ranks higher than Mike's at the time.

At IBM, he received an IBM Regional Manager's Award for successfully installing 13 systems in his rookie year in 1979. In these early days, he learned the value of using practical tools to improve his own productivity and others to achieve more.

Mike's first CIO role was with a small company in 1981 where he learned the value of getting things done through his team.

In 1983, Mike joined HBO & Company, a healthcare software products and services company serving hospitals throughout the United States. He helped develop HBOC's first PC software product and managed a startup organization created to explore the physician market. His management responsibilities grew as he managed the Eastern US installation and support operations of the company's mainstream products and had national responsibility for the company's three legacy systems. During his tenure at HBOC he was instrumental in improving the profitability of several product lines and helped the smooth transition of the company's staff from its legacy systems to newer technologies.

In 1990 Mike joined Medaphis Corp., a small healthcare billing services company. Mike managed the technologies of its largest division and helped the company grow from $30 million to $700 million in just 6 years. As the senior technology manager, Mike conducted due diligence and planned assimilation activity for more than 30 companies to support the company's phenomenal growth.

Mike has always been a manager that provided his time and effort toward mentoring and coaching others in order to help them achieve more. He gains a business perspective first and determines how to apply technology resources to help his company achieve its goals and objectives.

In November 2000, Mike decided to devote full time to his small entrepreneur company, MDE Enterprises, *www.mde.net*. MDE provides IT management training and consulting services. In order to reach more IT managers, he developed a plan and began writing the **IT Manager Development Series** in 2001. His writing style is a conversational style and "to the point". His objectives for the series were to provide meaningful material to IT managers throughout the world via Internet awareness and ordering capability that would help them achieve more. Before completing the last of ten publications on March 22, 2002 he had already sold over 1000 books to managers in 20 countries without spending any money on advertising.

Mike plans to add new content to the Series with new titles already defined. In addition, he released his **IT Manager ToolKit** in April 2002. The ToolKit is 80 tools that Mike has developed and used over the years to help him organize, monitor, and manage his IT organizations.

Mike shares a perspective that it took him 25 years of hard work and experience to be positioned to do what he does now with his own company. The result is that he now mentors and helps thousands of IT managers throughout the world with his material that is concise and presented in:

> **practical approaches** providing insight on
> **what to do** and **how to do it**
> with **examples** and
> **tools** to help any level IT manager ACHIEVE MORE.

Mike's IT management products and services can be found at *www.mde.net/cio*.

IT Management-101
Table of Contents

IT Management-101
Table of Contents (continued)

I. Understand Your Company's Needs

At any level of management position, it's paramount that you understand your company's goals and objectives. This shouldn't come as a surprise but you might be surprised at the number of managers that don't really take the time to do their homework and to understand the overall goal.

To understand what the company is trying to achieve is possibly more important for a manager of technology resources than for other managers of the company. The reason I suggest this is because your success or failure as an IT manager affects many others outside your department.

Take the time to understand your company's goals and objectives. Learn about their plans to accomplish them. Determine how these issues affect your role as a manager of technology. Depending upon your management level, you will be responsible for carrying out aspects of the plan or maybe even developing strategies that support the company's objectives.

How do you go about learning what you need to know? At a CIO level, you meet with senior managers of the company (CEO, CFO, COO, maybe even the Board of Directors) to develop an understanding. At a first line manager level, you spend time with senior managers of the technology organization to learn about company plans and objectives and hopefully the senior management of the company.

Depending upon your level, the company may not talk openly about specific elements of their plans but you certainly should be able to learn enough to know what the basic strategy for success is planned to be. For example, let's say that a company is planning to have significant growth by acquiring other companies that are similar to their own. Senior managers may know exactly who the specific targets are but they probably don't discuss them openly.

Even without specific targeted company acquisitions made known to you, you will be understand several issues:

A. Major growth is planned.
B. Growth is planned by acquiring other companies.
C. Other companies mean new employees and additional technologies to absorb.
D. Significant change is coming.
E. Additional employees place more strain on existing systems and infrastructure

Do you see what I'm getting to? You do not have to know all the specifics of the strategy to understand ramifications of a strategy. Junior managers should work with their senior IT managers to understand issues, develop strategy, and to prepare the appropriate plans necessary to support the company strategy.

Let's take a closer look at this issue.

A. Goals and Objectives

1. Focus initially in understanding what the company is trying to achieve. Every decision you make later should be supportive in one way or another to support your company's objectives.

2. Develop an understanding of key department objectives required to support the business.

3. Work with your senior IT managers to identify the IT objectives required to support the company and its key departments in meeting company goals.

4. Relate the IT organization objectives to your specific department responsibilities. Involve your senior IT managers as needed to develop a concise strategy that fully supports the company's plans. Using others that have more experience is actually a strength, not a weakness. Not doing so and failing to anticipate issues that are critical to success is a weakness.

B. Role needed for the IT Manager to Play

"You need me to manage, right?" The answer is not always a simple 'yes' or 'no'. Every IT organization has a unique set of dynamics. While there are definitely skills or traits that will work in most organizations, it's also important to understand the role that is needed in the specific position you have.

For example, an organization that is mature with sound processes in place and has experienced resources needs an entirely different management mindset than the organization struggling to find its way. Relate this to military terms and it's a difference in needing to 'take the beach' versus coming in later for the 'cleanup'.

Learning the type of management style needed for your specific IT organization early on helps you go about your work in the best manner possible to gain the results needed for the company.

When I pick up a new organization, I go about assessing what I have, defining the issues and challenges that exist, and developing the type of strategy needed to support my company to the fullest. You will better understand the management role you need to provide as you go through the assessment phase discussed next.

As you work through an assessment, you want to look for indicators that tell you the type of role needed. As you're learning about the company and it's IT needs, you're also looking for indications as to whether you are part of an "initial assault team" or the type of manager that just needs to fine-tune the existing organization.

II. <u>Assessment</u>

If you have read any of my other articles, you soon realize that I place a great deal of importance in assessing the situation. My management style is very much a "Ready, Aim, Fire" style of managing. I find it of major importance to know what you're firing at before you pull the trigger. This should not be much of a surprise, but there are too many managers that fire, then ask questions.

Ready , , , Aim , , , Fire!!

Assessing the issues is the first part – getting **Ready!!**

You should break an IT assessment phase into 4 parts:
      A. Senior Management Input
      B. Department Manager Input
      C. Client Input
      D. IT Staff Input

The following pages describe the process that I go through as I size up the IT issues of an organization. Additional information on assessment is included in my publication **What to Look For in a CIO.** You can view the Table of Contents of all my **IT Manager Development Series** at web site address *www.mde.net/cio* . There are similar concepts used in a few of the publications but all are written independently from the others (i.e., no cutting and pasting).

As you go through the interview process with senior management, department managers, clients, and finally the IT resources, your objective is to quantify the status of technology in four primary areas. If you are at a senior IT management level such as the CIO, you want to size up each area thoroughly. If you are a first level manager, focus in on the area that affects your primary responsibilities.

Another thing worth mentioning is that an IT assessment is as much of a business assessment as it is a technical assessment. I've seen so many organizations that have excellent technical skills but are not very productive for their company. The reason is almost always because they just don't get the business perspective they need to support their company fully.

The four areas of technology that I try to quantify and gain a clear understanding as I go through the assessment interviews are:

1. Infrastructure (Hardware systems, networks, telecommunications, desktops)
2. Business Applications (Software applications)
3. IT Staffing Organization
4. IT Processes (Change management, escalation, disaster recovery, client service, etc.)

These are the key parts of IT that must be addressed in order to have success in managing technology resources.

The interviews are conducted so that I can get a sense for each of these four areas and to begin developing a strategy for each. In order to do that, I have to assess the current status of each area and I generally place them into a mental category as follows:

1. Stable
2. Stable but needs attention for anticipated growth
3. Needs attention to achieve stability
4. Call 9-1-1

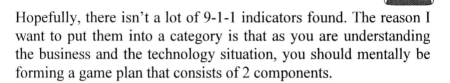

Hopefully, there isn't a lot of 9-1-1 indicators found. The reason I want to put them into a category is that as you are understanding the business and the technology situation, you should mentally be forming a game plan that consists of 2 components.

The first is a 90-day strategy. Your initial focus has to be placed on immediate needs and regardless of the maturity of the organization you're picking up, there will be immediate needs.

The second part of the game plan is a 12-18 month strategy. Similarly, regardless of the situation, there will be issues needing to be addressed that you can't attack right away.

More will be discussed on developing strategy later. My point here is that there is a real purpose for the interviews that you should have. That purpose is not just to learn; it is very much for you to start as quickly as you can in developing your management action plan and to develop rapport with key managers of the company. Realizing this as you enter your assessment interviews helps you position yourself to look for the issues that are there.

Again, managers of different levels will be more comfortable in this than others. First time managers are obviously going to be a little more cautious in taking an aggressive route and you rightfully should be. Take advantage of your senior IT manager or others with seasoned management experience to help you formulate and to validate your strategy as needed.

But, , , do not sit back and wait for your manager to tell you what to do! For what it's worth, I would always prefer to have an aggressive manager working for me that wants to push for results. It's much easier to direct that type of manager than it is to push the manager who waits for every task to be assigned. That's not managing!

Managing IT resources successfully is all about identifying your issues, prioritizing them, planning, communicating your plan, and implementing the plan.

There are a couple of key thoughts to understand at this juncture:

1. Anything can be done given the resource, money, and time.
2. I've never had the organization capable of doing everything that is needed as quickly as the user department or company would like to have it.

And you know what, you will probably never have all the technology resources needed to do everything that your users and clients would like to have. The main reason is that the cost would be prohibitive. That's why one of the key skills a successful manager must have is to be able to assess the business in determining the issues and developing priorities from that list. Often, the tougher challenge is to decide what you're 'not going to do', , , and to deliver the news to those who truly want it.

OK, enough of setting the stage. Let's get going with the assessment phase. We start with interviews with senior managers of the company.

Several tools are provided in MDE's **IT Manager ToolKit** to help you conduct IT assessments including questionnaires, guidelines, and templates to organize your findings.

A. Senior Management Input

We have all heard the phrase, "start at the top and work your way down". This has never been truer than when you are trying to assess IT issues, needs, and requirements. Depending upon the position you have as an IT Manager (first line manager versus a CIO position), the senior management you go to might vary. If possible, you want to hear from the very top of the business so there is no question as to what the goals and objectives of the company are.

Why is it important to understand the business mission and goals for the future?

    A. To determine what the IT issues are from senior management's perspective.

    B. To learn about the goals of the company so you can anticipate IT needs.

    C. To understand what senior management believes is working and not working in IT.

As mentioned earlier, senior management might be your CIO. If it is, it's still a good idea to try and have a conversation with other senior managers of the company such as the CEO, President, Senior VP's, COO, CFO, etc. The more you understand the roles and responsibilities of those that are running the company, the better.

When you sit down to have a conversation with any senior manager, there are a couple of things you will want to understand from their perspective. As you collect the data, look for:

- consistencies versus differing opinions
- level of dependency this manager places on IT
- satisfaction level with IT
- upcoming challenges that have IT requirements

I have performed these interviews so much that I don't use a guide, but I have included one in this book to help you with this part of assessment. The forms, questionnaires, etc. that I use to help you in this publication are annotated with comments, explanations, etc. to help clarify certain points. The Appendix includes blank forms that you can copy and use as you wish.

Senior Management Questionnaire
IT Assessment

Name: _____ Position: _____

Date: _____

1. **What is the company (or department) mission or purpose?**

    A. What does the company do?
    B. Is it a product company, service company?
    C. What industry are we in? (retail, professional, distribution, manufacturing, etc.)

    The purpose of this line of questioning is to better understand the core mission and objectives of the company (or department) day to day. As you interview departments within the company, you may find that some actually have revenue and profit requirements that might not be obvious. There may also be IT implications that are different or more significant than they are in this type of department in other companies. Bottom line is that as you listen to the input provided to your questions, you are looking for the issues that have technology implications and/or significance.

2. **Is the mission statement written and conveyed to all employees?**

> We are trying to determine whether or not the company (or department) has a defined mission statement and if so, whether employees are aware of and focused to it. Additional questions that bring this out will help you determine how well the company (or department) is focused to a single mission.
>
> It also gives you a sense of how strong senior management of the company (department) is in:
> - defining mission
> - communicating it to their employees
> - reinforcing it within the company (department)

3. **What is the company (or department) 3 to 5-year plan?**

A. Is there a long term plan?
B. How well defined is it?
C. How aggressive is it?

> In this area of questioning you want to determine what the plan is and what the implications are on the IT organization or the component of IT that you will be managing.

4. **What are the company (or department) growth plans/requirements for the next 12-18 months?**

A company planning to grow significantly has very different demands on technology than one with slow or no growth plans. Determining how fast the company will be growing will give you insight as to the dynamics of change expected to occur in the next year or so and the pressure that will be placed on IT infrastructure and services.

A company planning to double in size in the next 24 months potentially will have many more people than it does today. However, depending on the type of company and how it generates its revenue, it may not. It's important to understand the dynamics of revenue growth to people required to support that growth and where they exist in the company.

For example, a healthcare company that has clinics across the country likely almost doubles it's operations staff (clinic people) to double in size. Corporate support organizations will increase in size considerably as well unless there are key technology approaches that facilitate significant growth without adding people.

On the other hand, a software product company might be able to double revenue by adding additional software products or creating new markets. Support staff likely has to increase but possibly at a slower rate than the revenue growth.

5. How does the company (department) plan to achieve it's growth?

There are many different ways a company can achieve growth and the impact to IT is different. A company that increases sales of existing products or services places a very different requirement than a company that must develop more software products or services to achieve it's growth.

Likewise, a company that plans to achieve growth through acquisition of other companies places a truly unique set of circumstances for the IT organization. For one thing, the addition of more people throughout the company will increase at a much faster pace. There are also technologies and technology staff that must be dealt with and a strategy developed that assimilates them into the company or eliminates them altogether. Much more on this topic is discussed in publications dealing with IT Due Diligence and IT Assimilation.

Growth that comes in large chunks versus gradual growth has entirely different IT needs. The needs are similar, to be sure, but the pace and anticipation necessary to stay ahead of the power curve are very different.

6. How does technology fit into the company (or department) plans?

In this part you are trying to understand the relative importance that technology plays in the department's ability to achieve it's mission to support the overall company mission and plans. Look for indications that place heavy emphasis on technology in the following ways:

- mission critical role
- key growth issues
- product or service enhancement needs
- department training needs in the use of technology
- IT staffing or organization issues such as:
    - capacity
    - capability/skill
    - process that facilitates the needs
    - client service awareness

You also must assess whether IT is a support organization within the company or whether it is actually the primary revenue generating department. The dynamics of the two are obviously very different.

7. **What are the most important things that IT needs to focus on to support the company (department) business plans (both current and future)?**

As you enter this phase of questioning, you are essentially getting to the essence of how the senior manager feels about the company's technology resources. The manager should begin to open up and discuss any concerns or issues that exist as he/she looks at how technology is prepared to support it's mission and growth plans.

Look for impressions and expectations that the manager may have as well as the specific items identified in this part of the discussion.

8. **What dependencies does the company (or department) have on technology?**

Again, look for critical mission elements that require technology. When you complete this part, you want to have a good handle on the relative importance IT plays in helping the company (or department) accomplish its mission. In other words, "Is this a major client or a minor client?".

9. What are the company's (or department's) greatest challenges?

The obstacles or challenges the company faces will tell you a good bit about company culture, maturity, and it's ability to deal with major issues. A company trying to turn itself around and gain appropriate focus has much different needs than one that is trying to refine itself for incremental growth.

This discussion area will give you some sense as to the environment your IT organization is working in and helps you see quickly the level of issues the senior management team has identified.

10. How well are the technology resources supporting your business needs?

Be prepared to hear anything. Whatever the response is, take it with a grain of salt, but be sure to note it and understand that even if this impression is not appropriate, it is a valid impression that must be addressed later. If the input is negative, you have an opportunity. If the input is positive, you have an opportunity.

As you spend more time in the organization you will be able to better determine the appropriateness of the input. If it's appropriate, great. If not, your opportunity is to help the manager relate to appropriate IT service delivery as you work with his/her organization.

The reason for bringing this out is that in my experience I have worked with many, many department managers that thought they knew what their IT support organization role was, but in fact, they really did not know how to work with technology support resources and had very little expertise in knowing how to use the company's technology well.

Regardless, don't be too quick to agree or disagree with first impressions until you have time to hear more from others and observe the realities of what takes place. Just be certain to make a note on anything that appears to be "smoke". There may be a real "fire" underneath it all.

11. What are the IT organization's greatest challenges from your perspective?

You're looking for insight from the senior manager's point of view. You may get some very valuable input so don't take this input lightly. It's valuable input until you confirm it one way or another.

After you assimilate all the information from these interviews, you should have an excellent feel for the company's senior management perspective on it's IT organization. Knowing what the plans for the company's future are also positions you the best to begin your management responsibilities "in sync" with what the company needs.

HERE IT COMES!

Let's Get Acquainted!

B. Department Manager Input

With the department managers, you are essentially looking for similar input that you were getting from the senior managers. As you go through your discussions, you will receive input at a closer level of the actual activity occurring between IT and the user department. The input also allows you to confirm what you heard from senior management. Discrepancies should be noted and followed-up to the extent they have meaningful bearing on your management role in the company.

One other point. Depending upon the company mission and structure, your IT organization's customer may be the functional departments of the company (an 'internal' client). If so, treat them like a client and as the saying goes, "The customer is always right."

Let me emphasize that right here. **Even when the customer is wrong, he is right.**

No, I haven't fallen off a ladder and hurt my head. Nor have I forsaken the entire information technology community. What I mean is that if the customer's expectations are 'out of whack', it's still up to you as an IT manager to re-establish the appropriate expectation and to manage that expectation. The customer possibly (actually probably) isn't aware of what his/her expectation of IT should be.

Give each manager plenty of room to discuss his/her department, issues, challenges, concerns, etc. The more you can make them feel relaxed during the discussions the more insight you will be able to obtain. At this point, there are no wrong comments or answers.

You're also looking to develop partnerships with the other key managers in the company. Just as you will get a first impression of each of them, they are sizing you up as well. The best way I've found to make a positive first impression is to go into the interview prepared and be genuinely interested in their input. It's hard to fake it, so don't.

The department questionnaire that follows and the questions contained within it have been used by me for more many IT assessments. Use these and develop your own to create an interview process that works well with your own personality and management style.

Department Manager Questionnaire
IT Assessment

1. What is your department's primary mission/objective?

As you receive this input you will be able to start assessing how well the manager understands his business responsibility and how well he can articulate it. As you go through discussions with department managers, look for opportunities to develop strong relationships with those managers that have a heavy dependency upon IT.

2. To what extent do you depend upon IT support?

You're looking for the level of dependency the department has on IT and specifically for your responsible part of the IT organization.

As you work through all the departments of the company, you should be able to identify those departments that need IT support the most. You will also discover issues and challenges that might exist. While the interviews are proceeding you should be developing a mental picture as to where you need to be focusing close attention and your priorities should begin to start materializing in your mind.

3. What are your department's greatest challenges?

Many of these items may not be related to IT, but this information gives you insight into department/ company culture and work environment. You need to know about this as well in order to lead your team to successful performance levels.

4. What are the IT department's greatest challenges from your perspective?

The department manager may not have much insight, but you will probably get an opinion. If there is a common theme from several department managers, then you have some validation that it is probably accurate – at least from a technology user perspective.

Likewise, if one manager's comments are significantly different from several others, you may need to investigate a bit further to understand the real issue.

5. How well does IT meet it's commitments?

Commitments like:
- doing what they say they will do
- delivering projects on time
- delivering projects with minimal "breakage"
- follow-up
- working on the appropriate priorities
- responsiveness

Give the manager plenty of room to discuss this openly. Hopefully, it's good; if not, it spells opportunity for you as a new manager.

6. **Describe the responsiveness of the IT organization to your business needs.**

In this area, you want to determine whether the IT organization understands the meaning of client service, setting expectations with users, communicating effectively, and placing appropriate priority on issues that come up.

In addition, day to day support of technology requires that certain issues be escalated faster than others. For example, in most of my organizations we always had users that could not work without their systems up and running. If a critical server, telecommunications connection, or other issue prevented users from being able to access their system and do their work, it had to be escalated to my level (the CIO). The reason was that in troubleshooting the 'fix', I wanted to insure that all our options were being looked at and that it was an "all hands on deck" drill with all key IT resources focused as needed.

The bottom line is that I emphasized that there were no higher priorities when a critical system was down than to get that system back up and running.

7. **Do you have upcoming plans that depend upon technology for success?**

Having early indications of plans that impact your IT resources allows you to get ahead of the game. Anticipating needs is one of the more important things a manager needs to be able to do.

27

8. Describe your department's relationship with the IT organization.

> You're looking for alliances as well as problematic relationships between a department and IT. Both are opportunities and the better you are able to assess areas that need attention, the more you can take advantage of the 'honeymoon' period.

Don't underestimate the value of positive first impressions. The first 30-60 days in your new management role will have quite a lot to do with how other managers and their departments relate to you. You have a real opportunity to focus your organization's attention on key issues that are discovered in these interviews, and when others see positive things start to happen they will rally around your efforts.

C. Client Input

In this section, I refer to Client as an external client and not an internal company department that happens to be the IT organization's client. Companies that deliver software would have external clients, for example. If you do not work with external clients, you may want to skip this section.

Some of the same questions used with department managers are also pertinent here, but there are also other dynamics when dealing with external clients. For that reason, I include a separate questionnaire.

Much of this information can be gotten internally from your staff or other department managers. However, I can't emphasize strong enough that to get a true picture of how well you're supporting your external clients, you have to talk to them. Your IT department's perception is really not worth a whole lot right now.

You may think this very "criticizing" or prejudiced against IT organizations. I can assure you that I'm not; in fact, just the opposite. The reality is that the real perception you want to have initially is the client's. That is the only valuable perception of how well IT is handling the client at this point.

Make it a high priority to interview with a good cross section of your clients. Talk to those that love you and talk to the ones that are very disappointed with your business. You will probably find that the latter provides you the more valuable information. You may also find that some perceptions are "out of balance" with realistic IT support.

Did you say 'Opportunity' ?
The light just turned GREEN!!

You should visit the clients you want to interview if possible. I would not send a survey as I believe most clients don't pay a lot of attention to a survey. It's also very helpful to sit across the table from your client in their environment so you can read body language and gain as much insight as you can about the existing relationship - what's good, what's bad, issues, needs, etc.

You can learn a lot about a client by visiting his place of business.

You don't have to visit every client to size up the situation, but you do need to visit the bad or tough clients as well as a few good ones. Look for trends or consistencies in their message. After all, your goal with this exercise is to start developing an action plan to address key issues of your organization.

Problems are always opportunities!!

Client Questionnaire
IT Assessment

1. **How long have you been a client of _____?**

2. **Why did you buy their products or services?**

   You want to learn what led them to your company and what their original expectations were.

3. **Would you buy them again?**   **Explain.**

   This question gets you quickly to the client's satisfaction level – something you want to understand as soon as you can.

4. **Tell me about your business.**

   After you have insight as to satisfaction level, focus the client back to their business. Learning more about how the client views the business gives you more insight into their needs and the relationship it has with buying products and services from your company.

5. **How are priorities established with _____?**

   Find out how involved the client is with your company as requirements, priorities, and plans are developed. A client that is not very involved may have unrealistic expectations. A client that is involved with your company to establish a clear need and plan probably has appropriate expectations and can provide you with valuable insight.

6. How responsive is _____ to your business needs?

- Do we meet your needs?
- Do we meet deadlines?
- Do we deliver high quality items?
- Are we professional?
- Do we understand your concerns?
- Are we responsive when you have a problem?

By asking additional questions in this segment you should be able to get to the heart of any issues that exist and develop a mental picture of what the situation is with this client.

It is important to interview multiple clients so you can determine if the issues are systemic or an anomaly related to a particular client.

7. What are your greatest challenges as it relates to _____?

You are looking for insight and essentially recommendations from your client. Even a super happy client can give you areas of improvement – something that should always be part of a good manager's quest.

8. Do you have future plans that _____ should be anticipating?

Understanding potential needs and getting ahead of the issue as opposed to reacting is always a benefit to you as a manager.

9. **Does** _____ **understand your challenges, priorities, etc.?**

> This question will tell you whether the client believes your efforts are in sync with his needs. If not, you better get them in line or lose the client. If so, keep pushing those "right buttons".

10. **What are your recommendations to improve your relationship with** _____ **?**

> Even a great relationship can be improved. You should always be looking for ways to do a better job.

Many managers are often intimidated by an unhappy client. The trick to this and to become more comfortable in dealing with a problem client is to keep a few key thoughts in mind:
- it's not personal
- the client needs your help
- the client doesn't want to have a 'problem' discussion any more than you
- most clients are reasonable and will listen to options that help improve the situation
- you usually don't have to resolve the problem 'on the spot'
- a problem client is an opportunity

As a new manager of an IT organization, I relish the opportunity to meet with an unhappy client. It hasn't always been that way, but as my experience grew and I better understood the dynamics of a manager/client relationship it became much more comfortable.

Most clients actually need less than you might think to become "happy campers". You won't know until you sit down with them to find out. Assessments can be and should be fun.

D. IT Staff Input

Believe it or not, we finally do get to the IT staff to learn about their view of things. Before we begin with this part, let me say more about why I always talk to the IT resources last. It has been my experience that it is very typical for the IT organization and their client (whether that's external clients or internal company departments) to have very different opinions as to how well the IT department is performing.

Part of that is due to the fact that I have been pulled into many situations and companies that needed IT management help. In most cases, it's normal for the client and IT to have different perceptions of IT's performance, , , and for different reasons.

Nonetheless, a typical scenario goes like this. The client usually expresses a lack of focus, poor sense of urgency, and poor communication coming out of the IT department. The IT resources usually express that they work very hard, don't have the resources they need, and that the clients have unrealistic expectations of them.

$$2 + 2 = 5 \ ??$$

And you know what, , , they are probably both correct.

Back to my point. You should listen to the IT resources last so that you can approach senior management, department management, and client interviews with a totally open and unbiased mind (if there is such a thing). It doesn't do any good to develop a defense toward issues that the client might bring up. If you do, those interviews will not be well received.

Also, look for key points (smoke, if you will) that might suggest an area of improvement that's needed. When you get to the IT resources, you will inspect those areas to see if they actually exist, or whether it's more of a poor communication issue, or possibly an inappropriate expectation.

How about some examples?

1. If you hear, "IT never delivers software changes on time, and when they do it always breaks."

   Inspect the IT resources for good software change management processes, how they go about prioritizing software changes, how they communicate with their users on the status of changes, and how involved the client is in the QA process.

2. If you hear, "IT does not have a sense of urgency and they aren't responsive to my technology problems."

> Inspect for technology help desk processes, escalation guidelines, etc. Also look for morale issues and productivity problems.

3. When you hear, "Our systems have a lot of downtime."

> Inspect for infrastructure organization, security, and stability issues. Also look at the process used to implement changes to servers and services.

Obviously, these are general statements. In the interviews with those that suggest these issues exist, I ask questions that help me get specific situations or examples that I can use later to better understand the issue. Remember, these examples may only be smoke and not real problems. The problem might be resolved by simply communicating better. Until you learn more, you really can't tell.

Keep a list of what you consider to be important issues so you can get underneath the issue as you go through your IT resource interviews. It's extremely important that your questions lead you to specifics. Don't let the conversation end with general items — you can't grab smoke.

Ghosts are hard to catch as well!!

The lesson here is twofold:
1. You have to have specifics to work on.
2. You have to determine reality versus perception.

When called upon to conduct an IT assessment, it benefits me in that I've seen many organizations and while the specific dynamics are unique to each situation, there are usually many similarities as well.

Personal Note: *There are times when you can't talk to the client first to understand concerns or issues. Be careful that you don't predetermine the situation before you hear all sides.*

I managed a distributed technical support organization in the late 80's and one of my support groups was having major problems with one of its clients in Washington state. As head of the organization I decided to visit the client to determine what was needed to resolve the issues since they weren't paying their invoices.

Before I flew to Washington from my office in Atlanta, my support manager responsible for the account and I talked through the issues to provide me with some background. She was located in California. The input I received was that the client had a lot of internal organization problems and was a habitual complainer. A red flag went up when we didn't seem to have specific issues nor specific action plans to resolve the situation.

Upon meeting the client we all sat down to discuss the situation. After a bit of complaining, we were able to hone in on the specific issues with a bit of questioning that was targeted to get to the real issues and not just to hear general complaints. Part of the initial discussion was a fairly heated message from the client to me about our poor performance. My approach was to let the client get the issues off of their chest and to move the discussion to a set of specific issues that could be worked on. Sometimes you just have to let a client vent their frustration before you can get to the specifics. Don't take it personal because it really isn't.

I've never seen an organization be able to do much with generalities. You need tangible issues that can be addressed to improve a bad relationship.

After we finished the discussion and I had given the client another opportunity to add more, it was my turn to talk. At this point, I simply reduced the hour long message from the client to 4 key points that I picked up in the conversation. I listed the points and asked if I had gotten the essence of the issues or if there was something that I had missed. The client indicated that I had summed it up accurately.

**If you get this part accomplished, you're 70% to
a successful finish line!!**

Once the client agrees that you have understood their problem, now is a key part of the visit. I asked them that if I was able to address each of the four issues, would it resolve the problems that they were having with our company and justify getting current with their payments to us. I also mentioned that it might cost the client more money to resolve some of the issues but that I would be up front and tell them what we could do as well as what we could not do. I also asked the client to prioritize the issues in order of importance to their business.

The client agreed that depending upon our plan and how well we executed our action plan, it would indeed resolve our differences. I told the client that I would be back to them within a week with my recommendation and to expect a phone call at a designated time and date. We set the stage for a 3-way conference call with the client, the California support manager and myself.

The reason that I wanted to take some time was two-fold:

1. *I did not yet know how we would resolve one of the four issues.*
2. *I wanted the client to know we were putting real thought into the problem and that it was not just a quick fix from Atlanta. It was important to support the California manager who had responsibility to support the client in the future.*

The solution eventually worked and it did cost the client more money every month. They were happy to pay it to achieve positive results. Within a year they were buying more products from our company.

So what was the problem? The problem was essentially two parts:
1. *The support manager was listening, but not hearing the client and getting to specific issues.*
2. *The support approach being used for this client was a bad fit for their personality and needs. Every client has its own personality and what works for one may not be effective for another. Managing technology resources is often as much about understanding dynamics of a situation as it is understanding the technical aspects.*

Creating success from a bad situation is actually simple:

- Understand the real issue.
- Gain agreement that the real issues are identified.
- Develop an appropriate plan with room to deliver high quality and in a timely manner.
- Communicate the plan and gain concurrence.
- Deliver what you say you will and when you say you will.
- Communicate obstacles or problems as early as possible.

More on this later, but my point is that it's pretty easy to be a successful IT manager if you have the right road map and you execute it properly.

Before we go forward, we should acknowledge that there are clients that simply like to beat up their vendors. We've all had them. These clients (whether they are external clients or internal company department heads) are actually far and few between – truly exceptions. Most of the time, the "bad client" is a stereotype applied to that client that expects to receive quality service from a responsive IT organization and tells you about it.

In my opinion, that's not only appropriate, it's the right thing to expect. Don't you expect that from companies you buy from?

The reason for the misunderstanding is that IT is usually not doing an effective job of quantifying the issues, gaining agreement with the client, or is failing to deliver upon commitments.

Very solvable!!

The questions I normally ask when conducting an interview with the IT staff is provided on the following pages.

IT Staff Questionnaire
IT Assessment

1. How long have you been with the company?

This question and the rest are important to develop understanding of background, experience, and maturity.

2. What did you do before joining the company?

Previous experience means a lot – understand who you have in front of you.

3. Describe your current responsibilities.

Very quickly you will learn how well this has been defined by previous management and how well each resource understands it.

4. What do you like about your current position?

People work harder when they like aspects of their job. They also tend to work on the things they like. If you heard in earlier interviews from sources outside of IT that there were issues that this resource should be addressing, look for insight to understand a couple of things:
1. Does the resource know there is an issue?
2. Does the resource see it as an issue that should be addressed?
3. Is the resource addressing the issue?
4. How is the issue being addressed?
5. Does it have the right priority placed on it?

5. **What do you dislike about your current position?**

> You might learn a lot about the person, the organization, the client, the company, and previous management style in this part. Keep an open mind!!

6. **How would you describe your department's mission?**

> Look for appropriateness, knowledge of the resource in understanding it, and whether or not the person believes in it.

7. **How well do you believe the IT department is meeting it's objectives?**

> Look for how the department (resource) feels about itself, how well they understand their mission, and do they understand the meaning of client service and how to go about delivering IT products and services, etc.

> You also want to determine if this impression is the same as what you've heard from clients and managers of other parts of the company.

8. **What are the major challenges of your department?**

> Look for repeated issues from earlier interviews.

9. What do you see as the company's key challenges?

With this question, you're going to hear about issues the person believes to be important within his/her company. It may be an issue that's a perception and not real. Keep in mind that if the employee tells you about it, it is a real issue to them even if they have the wrong understanding. At any rate, you should receive valuable insight into the company, the employee, or both.

10. Who is your client and tell me about them?

You better find out if the employee actually knows who the client is and if so, what the client's challenges and needs are.

11. What do you want to be when you grow up?

Be prepared for anything. It's important for an employee to know that you're interested in understanding where they want to get to. You may have an employee that thought they should be in your new position. If so, that can be good.

A strong manager understands his assets (resources) and develops a plan to help them advance. You don't have to have it all figured out today, but you had better be looking at how you can help your resources achieve their objectives soon. The answer you get in this interview may not be appropriate, time will tell.

For example, I've had people tell me in the initial interview that they wanted to be the manager of the group. After they better understood what being a real manager entails, most changed their minds.

As the manager, I always want to empower people and let them seek their own level and to "be all they can be".

12. What are the top 3 things you'd like to see improved or changed?

This can be in the company, in the department, or just in general. Let them tell you what they want.

13. When was your last review and salary increase?

If you have picked up an organization where this was not paid attention to, you should look at it and see what you can do quickly, especially your key people.

14. How does management measure your performance?

You want to learn how the company, especially the IT department goes about performance planning and reviews. Feedback is important to detail oriented technical people.

Regardless of company culture, it's important to create performance plans for IT staff, to do annual reviews at a minimum, and to have career planning discussions. In today's business environment, it's too easy for your best employees to go to another company. If you do a few things well, you won't have a lot of turnover.

III. Key Questions That Must Be Answered

OK, you have interviewed every person that comes into contact with technology in your company. Just kidding. You do need to interview all key managers of the company, a good sampling of external clients, if any, and your IT resources.

As you were interviewing and discovering everything you can about the company, there are a few questions that you need to be able to answer. You have just completed the major part of discovery. Now it is time to start developing your plans. Before you do, answer these questions:

1. *Is there a plan for your area of responsibility?*

> It is very hard to achieve success without a plan. If none exists, I suggest you develop one soon. We will discuss more on that topic later.

2. *If a plan exists, does it appear to be appropriate for the issues you've discovered?*

> You always want to do the right things. Only then should you focus on doing things right. If the plan is focused on issues that do not fit the conclusions you gained from the interviews, step back and determine if it should be changed. Better to achieve the results that's really needed for the company and your clients than to complete a plan that looks good but brings little value.

Personal Note: *In one company situation, I entered into a scenario where the company had just gone through a 12-month beta test of a new software application. They had spent about $1.5 million dollars in development costs and a lot of time and effort. It had been installed in about 10% of the company.*

After the interviews and assessing the issues surrounding the application, it was clear that the company should not invest another $1.5 million to implement it across the rest of the company. There were significant risks in being able to scale the product in a company that was expecting to have major growth plus the sheer cost at that time was beyond what the company could afford to do in that area of the business.

There were numerous issues related to support and while the product seemed to have "sizzle" in theory, it did nothing to improve profitability or cash flow for the company.

Delaying the project was not a popular position to take with the few users that had been the beta test, but it was the right decision given the situation and helped position the company for the growth that they wanted to achieve.

3. Does your organization understand client service and do they perform their duties in a manner that shows that they do?

Hopefully, they do. If not, you have a cultural change that must be introduced to your organization. My thoughts along this line have always been, "The only reason we have a job in IT is because there are clients that need technology to do their jobs and need our expertise and help."

It's a simple but very appropriate principle to follow.

4. How are priorities determined?

The answer to this question tells you whether the IT agenda is its own or that of its clients. Priorities need to be driven by client needs, not IT desires.

5. Is the organization working on the right priorities?

Are the projects being worked on today consistent with what you heard from senior management, department managers, and clients needs? If not, you probably need to reassess the appropriateness of the projects in question. At a minimum, get an agreement from those that should be driving your priorities to insure they still want the questionable projects completed.

I

6. *s there a change management process for implementing technology changes and does it work?*

> If interviews are telling you that IT misses deadlines and has a lot of breakage when technology changes are implemented, the answer is probably 'no' or the implementation process that is in place is very loose. Either can be fixed and the results will be improved performance and higher productivity.

7. *Does the IT organization communicate effectively with it's clients?*

> Hopefully, clients know what IT organizations are doing when it affects them and they are not hit by a lot of surprises. Most successful business people do not like surprises.

8. *What are the immediate needs?*

> Break this down by client areas such as accounting, operations, payroll, etc. As you identify the pressing needs you will want to place a weighting factor of some type on each issue to help you prioritize them later.

9. *Does the organization anticipate and plan or react?*

> Understanding whether you've entered an organization that anticipates and plans versus reacts to situations is important.

> An IT organization has to have 'firefighters' but the organization needs to be in the business of 'preventing fires'.

If it is a reactionary organization, you will want to do things that helps it get ahead of the power curve. Even a help desk organization that answers support questions every day can do things that reduces problems and helps the users become more self sufficient, thereby preventing more than reacting.

There are actually two different things you're assessing as you go through this process. On the one hand, you want to understand what the right technical issues are and the projects that are underway. On the other hand, you have to determine how professional and experienced the organization is in delivering IT products and services. The combination of these two parts makes for a well balanced approach.

Neither part can be very effective without the other part. You can have the most technical expertise available but if those resources do not know how to prioritize and communicate effectively with your clients, so what? Conversely, you won't get very far with just good manners and smooth talking without capable technical expertise. In my opinion, both are equally important.

Sidebar: *In my experience you can usually get by with weaker technical expertise than without the client service skills. An ability to prioritize, manage expectations, and communicate well can often overcome the lack of heavy technical expertise. I have certainly seen extremely strong technical people be ineffective because they did not have communication and project management skills.*

IV.   Establish First 90-Day Objectives

It's time to start putting plans on paper. It's not a plan if it is not written down. If it isn't worth the time to write it down and communicate it to others, then it probably isn't worth doing.

I recommend you approach planning the management of IT resources in two distinct ways. There are short term, immediate issues that should be addressed and long term issues. My first set of objectives will always be a 30 – 90 day plan. This short term plan will also always be approached in a manner to support long range objectives.

It's important to make a note here. You will know more about the long term strategy needed after a few months. The best assessment will not provide you with enough insight to develop a bullet proof long term strategy 'right out of the gate'. Planning is an evolving element and not just a static thing.

This is not to suggest that plans are so dynamic that they are constantly changing radically. However, they do change and should as the business dynamics evolve and as you become more attune to the needs of the company.

How do you go about developing your first 90-day plan?

With time and experience, it actually becomes a second sense as to what the priorities need to be after going through the assessments. For this exercise, we will take a little more structured approach.

First thing to do is to establish where you believe the organization you are responsible for is today and where it needs to be in 12 – 24 months. As mentioned earlier, any short term plan has to support a long term plan. Otherwise, you may have to pull pieces out or rework them because you did not approach the short term issues in a way that supports your long term goals.

To do that, refer back to the elements that you needed to be looking for and understanding in your assessments. They are:

- Infrastructure
- Business applications
- IT staffing organization
- IT processes

And your assessment of these major IT components need to be viewed in context of:

- Company goals
- Client needs
- Available capital

There are many factors surrounding or affecting any planning that you need to do. The graphic below shows there are diverse issues that have to be accounted for as you develop your plan.

IT Planning "Influencers"

All of these elements have a bearing on how you put your plans together. As mentioned before, every IT management situation has different dynamics. While most situations require planning and solid execution to be a success, every situation is unique as you look to develop the first 90-day plan.

By the way, this certainly is not all of the issues that can influence your planning.

You should also know that there will be many different routes that you can take to reach your objective. There are many ways to "skin a cat" as they say.

Personal Note: *I have worked with one individual off and on for over 15 years. He and I have very different managerial approaches, but we have often discussed, even laughed about getting to the same objective through very different paths.*

So, 'you take the high road and I'll take the low road'. We both will arrive in 'Scotland' as the old song goes. The objective is not necessarily getting there first. Successful managers get there predictably and 'as planned'.

Predictability and 'as planned' is worth a lot to most companies.

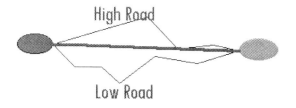

The mythical straight line to reach an objective is the
quickest path but rarely happens.

Let's say you've inherited a Client Support Desk as the new manager. As you went through all the interviews and reached your assessment, you identified 10 issues that needed to be addressed. And let's say that 3 of those issues were all very important and you aren't sure which needs to take highest priority.

If possible, start them all assuming the resources are available. If one is a prerequisite to other issues, then that more or less dictates that it has to be a higher priority. You also should be validating your initiatives with stakeholders of the company so you know that your priorities are their priorities.

Sidebar: *You're a new Client Support Desk Manager. In the assessments you determined that you have the following issues that need to be addressed in the next 90 days:*
  - *Hire an additional support desk resource*
  - *Develop a call tracking database*
  - *Develop call trend reports for management analysis*
  - *Train the existing support desk on a specific software application*
  - *Buy new PC for the new hire*
  - *Develop and implement escalation procedures*
  - *Develop client support service level agreements (SLA's) and communicate to clients*
  - *Train the staff on tracking and analyzing support calls*
  - *Conduct employee "preventive issues brainstorming session"*
  - *Plan the training of the support desk resources for a new product to be released in 6 months*

Taking a generic list and placing priorities on them is simpler than most think. It's actually as much common sense as anything. To help you, lets use a simple matrix that assists in determining the priorities in our example. Once the priorities are known, the plan materializes pretty much on its own. I've placed the tasks from the list above into a decision matrix that should help you develop the priorities of this example.

Issues Priority Matrix Sample

Pri.	Task	Est. $$	Lead time	Prereq.	Dependencies
1	Hire new support resource	$10,000	30 days		- recruiting dollars available - position and salary approved
2	Develop call tracking database	$6,000	days	9	- definition of database elements - reporting needs
3	Develop call trend reports	$2,500	45 days	2,9	- report design
4	Train staff on business application	0	14 days	9	- business application expertise - training agenda and materials
5	Buy new PC	$1,000	7 days		- capital request approval - new hire approved
6	Develop/implement escalation procedures	0	7 days	9	
7	Develop/implement SLA's	0	30 days	9	
8	Train staff on call tracking procedures	0	60 days	2,3	- call tracking database
9	Conduct "brainstorming session"	0	7 days		- develop agenda to facilitate
10	Plan new product training	0	90 days		

As you can see, we simply put the tasks into the table and added columns for relevant issues that might have a bearing on the timing of executing each of the tasks. Similar to building a project plan, we include prerequisites and dependencies (or constraints). As we analyze the "to-do's", the objective of this step is to reach a definitive priority for each task, or another way to say it is to define the path sequence in which we can execute each of these tasks to reach our objectives.

Now that we have added the associated costs, lead times, prerequisites, and dependencies, we can go back to each task and place a priority. The approach that I usually use is to put a priority number beside the task in the Priority column. If two items can be accomplished simultaneously, I'll use the same priority number. As with this simple example and others, you could end up with 4 different plans that would work. That's perfectly reasonable.

For now, let's go to the table and place a priority on each task.

#	Pri.	Task	Est. $$	Lead time	Prereq.	Dependencies
1	1	Hire new support resource	$10,000	30 days		- recruiting dollars available - position and salary approved
2	1	Develop call tracking database	$6,000	30 days	9	- definition of database elements - reporting needs
3	2	Develop call trend reports	$2,500	45 days	2,9	- report design
4	1	Train staff on business application	0	14 days	9	- business application expertise - training agenda and materials
5	2	Buy new PC	$1,000	7 days	1	- capital request approval - new hire approved
6	2	Develop/implement escalation procedures	0	7 days	9	- defining critical escalation points
7	3	Develop/implement SLA's	0	30 days	6,9	
8	3	Train staff on call tracking procedures	0	60 days	2,3	- call tracking database
9	1	Conduct "brainstorming session"	0	7 days		- develop agenda to facilitate
10	4	Plan new product training	0	90 days		

In our example, you see that I only have 4 real priorities out of 10 tasks. What I did as I went through the list was to place each item into a 'timing phase' of when I would expect to execute the task. With this example, it looked to be basically one of four phases of implementation. Now that I have this part defined, I can draw a picture. Being visual helps me and others understand the plan, timelines, and prerequisites much quicker.

Sample Client Support Desk 90-Day Plan

Phase-I	Phase-II	Phase-III	Phase-IV

Phase-I
1. Hire new Support Resource
2. Develop call tracking database
4. Train staff on business application
9. Conduct "brainstorming" session

Phase-II
5. Buy new PC
3. Develop call trend reports
6. Develop/ implement escalation procedures

Phase-III
8. Train staff on call tracking procedures and new tools
7. Develop/ implement Service Level Agreements (SLA's)

Phase-IV
10. Develop new application training plan

90 days

60 days

There is quite a bit of flexibility in lining up each task as long as you accomplish the prerequisite tasks first.

As you go through the assessments for your particular situation, there should be some very specific needs identified that are on the critical path. It might be finishing an active project, adding capability in a software application, or simply getting e-mail in place.

Regardless of how you approach it, there are a few "influencers" that should always take priority. Client needs, company plans, and expense influences must always be at or near the top of your evaluation. If you have a lot of immediate challenges, you have to break them into pieces and to establish priorities that buy time by hitting the most urgent needs of the client and/or company first.

In general, there is a hierarchy within IT that must be followed to be truly successful. If you build your business on a weak IT structure, it ultimately topples with growth. This is such an important issue that we devote a whole section to it titled **First Things First**. Normally, I would wait to get into that section but part of the concept needs to come out here.

Developing a 90-day plan and a 1-year plan has to tie to a basic understanding that you must develop a strong and stable framework before you focus on the strategic projects. If the company does not have stable, reliable systems in place, placing strategic projects on top of them will only cause the crash that ultimately happens to be louder and quicker.

We need a picture:

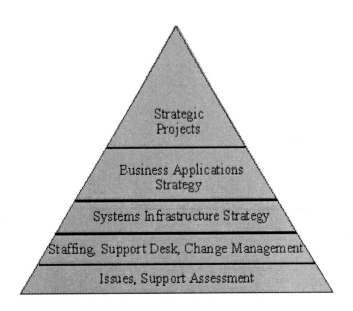

IT Project Priority Hierarchy

As a CIO, I have always managed from a principal that to achieve consistent results, you have to insure you have a solid foundation to work from. Look at the pyramid example above to better understand. The approach I highly recommend, is to begin at the 'ground floor'.

In this publication, we have spent time so far in discussing the first layer – assessment and identifying the issues. The next layer has to do with IT processes and the IT organization's ability to support the technology of the company.

Follow with the systems infrastructure and the business applications layers and then, and only then, are you really prepared to go after real strategic projects. In the section you will read later titled **First Things First**, we will go into more detail. The point I'm making here is that you should have this concept in the back of your mind as you're developing your 90-day issues list and developing priorities for them.

If you think back to the Support Desk example we used, the real objective that we wanted to get to was to position the organization to support a major new application that was to be released in 6 months. As we assessed this part of the IT business, it also became apparent that we would be short staffed and that the current support approach needed improvement. So, our plan actually went through many steps just to get to the part we wanted to get to – developing the new application support plan.

Going straight to the strategic task that we want to accomplish without having a solid foundation only creates a bigger challenge to fix later on. Remember the old Bardahl oil commercial, "Pay me now, or pay me later."? This message is very true in managing IT resources.

V. 1-Year Game Plan

The 90-day game plan focused on urgent issues as you might expect. The 1-year plan is more strategic in scope. Don't get hung up on developing a 1-year versus 2-year plan. The further out the plan the more you will probably "tweak" it over time. At the very least, develop a plan for the next year. The key is to establish a big picture of the direction you plan to take and the key projects that will be required to get you to your <u>stated destination</u>.

If you expect your short term plans to compliment and to support a longer range vision, you have to have one. Otherwise, you will implement projects that conflict with the long range plan.

Did I say, "stated destination"? You bet I did!! No plan is worth much unless you clearly state your destination (objectives) and document them.

Also remember, there are no rules as to how long it should take to stabilize your part of the IT business before you are able to take on strategic projects. Depending upon the situation, it may already be very stable and waiting for you to 'go', or it may take several months to clean up a real mess.

"What it is , , , is what it is!!"

By stating your 12-month (or more) plan objectives, you are also giving senior managers and clients the opportunity to validate your objectives. One of the worst things an IT manager can do is to work in a vacuum and avoid communicating where he is going and what he's working on. We see this time and again and it probably has as much more to do with dissatisfaction with IT organizations than any other thing – even above poor performance.

You will hear me say this over and over, but I'm convinced that managing the client's expectations is **the key** to successful IT performance.

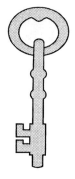

All right, the first step is to define two things.
1. Define where you are.
2. State where you want to be a year or more out.

Step 1 – Defining where you are is essentially quantifying the issues that exist as you have conducted your assessments. You should also do a quick inventory of your organization. A simple list will do – hit key items that are important for your particular responsibility. Over the years, I have found the list included in the table below to apply to most situations.

IT Organization Inventory

Item	Assessment	Comments
Staff capacity		
Staff experience/skill		
Client service awareness		
Appropriate tools available		
Change management processes		
Systems stability		
Project management skills		
Industry/business knowledge		

Item ---------- List of key skills, tools, etc. needed for the organization to do the job well.

Assessment – I usually go with *Low, Medium, High.*

Comments --- Clarify the challenge, identify a specific need or item that solves the issue.

Step 2 – Defining where you want to be a year or more out has a lot to do with what you've heard senior managers tell you in the assessments. It should also include input from other senior IT manager's insight into what you're going to need to have the organization positioned for in the future.

Developing strategic IT plans requires experience, an understanding of the business, and vision. Many find this difficult. It certainly can be, but I believe that it has more to do with the necessity to sit down and to think through the issues more than anything else. Planning takes time and proactive work. Real work!! Most of us are more comfortable reacting to issues than being proactive. It's easier to react but it makes it harder to have a successful organization.

Companies and people want and need leadership. Proactive planning, stating your vision, and executing from a plan shows real leadership. Try it and I can assure you will see positive results because most of your counterparts are working reactively, not proactively.

Depending upon the situation you have with your organization responsibility, this plan will vary considerably. If you are a programming manager, it will likely deal with application functionality to a great extent. If you manage the infrastructure of your company, it will include projects that continue to add stability, capacity, additional services and security of your systems. A CIO should include all parts of the IT business responsibility.

Need a picture? The following is an example of a 12-18 month plan that was developed to help a company move from a manual billing company to an automated billing company. This particular part of the plan includes elements of business applications and infrastructure. "The names have been changed to protect the innocent."

Business Automation Strategy
11/13/00

6 Steps to a "Paperless" Environment

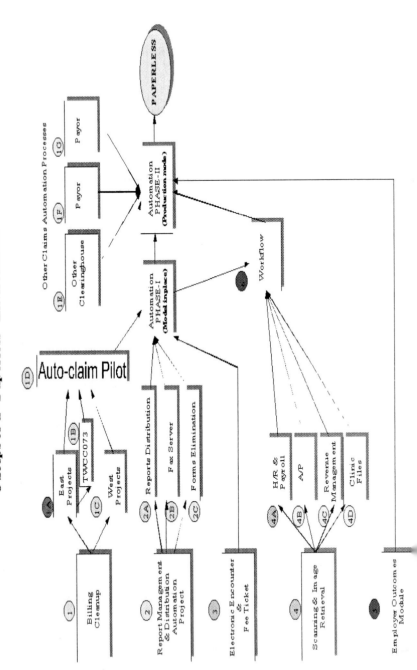

Several points are worth mentioning:

- This plan includes mostly strategic projects
- The plan could not be embarked upon until many stabilizing projects were previously completed.
- Many of the projects are taking place simultaneously as you can see. The key is to insure that projects are addressed in such a way as to compliment each other and to anticipate other project needs.
- I broke the plan into 6 major projects. Sub-projects are identified as well.
- This particular plan impacts many departments and will require significant planning, coordination, and communication.

Why do you create a visual plan?

There are actually several reasons.

1. Define the plan to others.
2. Gain agreement from 'stakeholders' that this is the appropriate plan.
3. Establish with others that it involves quite a bit of effort and commitment.
4. Shows dependencies and a requirement of coordination.
5. Helps clients and IT employees see and understand your vision.

The best way I have seen to manage other people's expectations is to put your plans on paper and to cover it with them. It provides the perfect way to gain concurrence or to get input that allows you to change the plan as needed to meet their expectations.

VI.   First Things First

As you develop your plans for your area of responsibility, you have to address "first things first". The best way I know how to develop this idea with you is to use an example of an IT manager that becomes a CIO for a company. With the CIO position, you have to take all aspects of the technology support delivery for a company into perspective. We will go through a high level thought process that a CIO has to work through to develop an overall strategy for the company.

We spent a lot of time discussing the assessment phase of developing an IT strategy, or plan. Getting as clear of a picture of where you are and where the company wants to be is as important as anything you can do. It's very hard to hit the target if you don't know what you're shooting at and what tools you have to shoot with.

Sidebar: *Let's take this 'shooting' analogy a bit further. If you're preparing to "shoot" something, it might help you to know:*
1. *What you're shooting at , or "where you want to go":*
   - *is the target moving*
   - *how fast is the target moving*
   - *how far away is the target*
   - *how large is the target*

   With the information above, it's easier to determine what type of weapon you might need to hit your target. You must understand the objective to determine what tools you're going to need.

2. *What are your skills, or "where are you now".*
    -   *do you have the proper equipment*
    -   *are you trained to use the equipment*
    -   *is the equipment properly set up*

Clearly defining the objective and truly understanding what you have to work with initially gives you the essential pieces by which to develop a game plan that has a high likelihood of success. The plan simply fills in the gap with a logical set of progressions so that you achieve your result.

Current   Goal
status

And remember, there rarely exists a straight line "from here" to "the objective".

The objective of the assessment was to:
    -   determine where the company wants to go – **the goal**
    -   determine the state of technology services today – **the starting point**
    -   begin identifying the issues that must be addressed to achieve the goal – **the plan**

As we discussed earlier, the manager must start with a very tactical (30-90 day) plan that puts the organization into position as quickly as possible to take on larger objectives that lead to reaching the goal.

At a CIO level, the entire technology requirements of the company must be reviewed, analyzed, and a plan developed for each area that supports every part of the IT organization leading to the overall objectives. There will be competing needs for IT resources from the company, and possibly even within the IT organization. When a CIO creates his/her plan to develop the IT services needed for the company's overall objective, there is a hierarchy that must be followed.

We looked at this hierarchy earlier. Let's take a closer look:

When a CIO does his assessment, there is a long list of items that are discovered:

Where we are	Where we want to be
Client service capability	Size of company
Change management process	Growth plans
IT services being provided	Business requirements of the future company
Quality of IT services being delivered	Key technology advances required
Growth capacity of IT services	Differences in future client needs
Staff strengths and weaknesses	New product or service lines required
Staff skill gaps	Productivity gains facilitated by technology
Infrastructure status	Cost of IT as a per cent of revenue
Data center security	
User capability in using technology	
Support desk status and issues	
Support problem trends and issues	
Problem escalation procedures	
Business applications status	
Business application needs	
Project management capabilities	

This is by far a 'short list' of all the issues that will be discovered. The point is that the assessment includes a very disperse set of issues. In order to achieve the goals of the company, most, if not all, of these issues must be addressed to compliment the overall plan that will lead to success. It will be virtually impossible to take care of all issues simultaneously. An effective CIO will establish a set of priorities that follows the hierarchy we showed in the IT **Project Priority Hierarchy**.

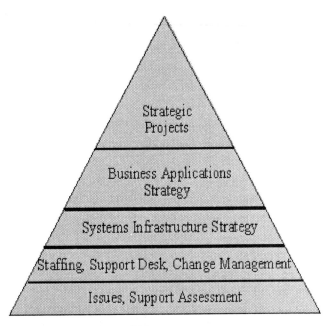

IT Project Priority Hierarchy

The goal of any real CIO is to work on strategic projects (the part that sits atop the pyramid structure in our diagram). Those projects might be the introduction of totally new products or services that have a major impact on productivity of the company or it might be to assimilate the technologies of acquired companies. Either way, the CEO and other senior managers are eager to get to the part that helps really improve or grow their business.

It would be nice to be able to just go straight for the "gusto". Unfortunately, it's not normally a straight line as mentioned now at least 4 times.

The reason we spent so much time on assessment is that the assessment makes up the very foundation that you will build all your objectives on. You will tweak those plans over time but the major pieces of the plan will probably stay intact if you've done a good job in assessing the situation.

OK, the race is on! We want to get to some strategic projects (the top of the pyramid) as soon as possible. We also want to be able to have a very sound foundation by which to develop and support new technologies, one that is not only stable but scalable.

It works like this:

- You can't fix or improve anything if you don't know what the issues are.
  (Assessment)
- You can't make changes if you don't understand the problems, have capable staff to do the work, and have a sound change management process in place.
  (Staffing, Support Desk, and Change Management)
- It's very hard to develop software applications without solid systems infrastructure.
  (Systems Infrastructure Strategy)
- Before taking on strategic projects, you need to have stable applications in place.
  (Business Applications Strategy)
- Finally, we get to strategic project work.

This does not imply that many parts of this hierarchy cannot be worked on at the same time. In fact, much of it does get worked on simultaneously. What is emphasized is that before you develop your Business Application strategy, you should have put your infrastructure game plan together.

It's also important to note that when you develop the Infrastructure Strategy, you must consider elements that will be required for your business applications such as:

- what the business applications and technology services will be
- number of users that will be using the applications
- locations of the users
- security implications
- etc.

A strategy, as I define it, is creating the high level plan on how you will achieve the objective. You don't have to know how you will achieve your Business Applications Strategy needs when you create your Infrastructure Strategy, but it certainly helps to know what the applications and services are that will be needed for the infrastructure to support. If you are not sure, it should automatically tell you that your Infrastructure Strategy must be somewhat open in order to add critical applications determined at a later date or to scale in size to support an undetermined user base.

Let's take a closer look at each layer of the IT Project Hierarchy illustration:

1. **Assessment** – As mentioned over and over, this is a critical stage to insure that you are directing IT resources in the right places to:

   - achieve company goals
   - fill resource gaps
   - position systems for growth and stability
   - establish a quality delivery of services
   - complete projects that have value for the business

2. **Support Desk, Staffing, Change Management Process** – This layer focuses quickly on three key areas that are important for any successful IT organization:

   A. ***Support Desk*** – It's critical that the CIO establish a quick process to provide base level support for infrastructure (systems) issues and business applications issues. Creating a functional support desk (assuming none exists) to support user challenges and needs in these two areas does two important things:
      1) Improves day to day support
      2) Starts gathering information that will tell you what the problems are.

   B. ***Staffing*** – Start sizing up staffing needs right away to resolve issues such as:
      - capacity
      - skill gaps
      - bench strength (backup) for key skills

   Hiring new staff has to be balanced with budget availability and your ability to define the job. A good CIO is always lining up the staff needed to move the organization to the next level and knows well in advance of hiring the skill sets that will be needed.

   You always want to try to hire proactively in a manner that anticipates needs of the company. You should try to avoid hiring defensively or in a reactionary manner.

I also recommend that you hire strong, motivated candidates. I would always prefer to manage a few senior level people that are very capable, may make a lot of money, and outperform a staff that's 25% larger. It's usually cheaper and a lot more fun to manage because you'll be more successful.

Much more is discussed on this topic in the publication titled, **Building a Successful IT Organization**.

C. *Change Management Process* – If you are to implement change to the company by completing new projects, you must have sound change management processes in place.

Even if the goal is simply to maintain existing systems and applications, you still need to manage changes effectively. Otherwise, the support delivery of your IT team(s) will be unpredictable and will likely incur a good bit of breakage.

3. **Infrastructure Strategy** – Define your plan for each part of the company's infrastructure and the timing of each key project. Infrastructure requirements include addressing each of the components listed below. As you build a game plan for each, the plan should include elements that address capacity, functionality, security, backup, recovery, redundancy, support, scalability, and standards.

  A. System server needs (for business applications)
  B. Network server needs
  C. E-mail standards and address naming convention
  D. Remote connectivity architecture
      - dial-up
      - wide area network (WAN)
      - local area networks (LAN)
      - other connectivity
  E. Network monitoring and support
  F. Internet connectivity and usage
  G. Intranet connectivity and usage
  H. IP addressing standards
  I. Data center
  J. Security
      - systems
      - networks
      - applications
      - physical facilities
      - remote access
  K. PC's & supported PC application software
  L. Printing standards
  M. Fax server
  N. Printing distribution capabilities
  O. Backup and off-site storage
  P. Data center operations
  Q. Disaster recovery
  R. Phone systems (voice)

S. Support desk and escalation procedures
T. Change management process
U. Infrastructure systems diagram & maintenance
V. Technology assets inventory
W. Software license inventory and compliance
X. Systems tools

4. **Business Applications Strategy** – Addressing functionality needs of business departments and/or your external clients are very important. I don't need to tell you that, though. As you begin developing and implementing plans on the lower levels, you may also be getting into needs of this layer as well, especially if urgent needs or gaps in your business applications exist.

In most cases, the resources that focus on the business applications are different than those that work on networks, and hardware issues. This makes it very reasonable to focus resources on both layers at the same time. The key is that the infrastructure team has to be laying the groundwork for the business applications to have adequate systems and connectivity to function as needed.

It's sort of like laying the rails before the train can move down the track.

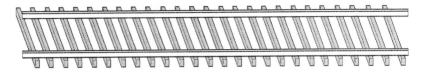

Laying groundwork is not the most exciting or fun work to do, but just as the train has to have the track, business application enhancements have to have the infrastructure that supports them.

5. **Strategic Projects** – The quickest approach to implement key projects that provide excellent return for the company is not necessarily, nor normally, to go right to the strategic project and begin implementing. OK, already; that's the last time I mention the 'straight line' concept. I promise.

Always remember that if you build your foundation on wobbly legs, the full success of implementing a strategic project is going to be minimized.

Let me explain a bit. Let's assume that a strategic objective is to assimilate acquired company technologies as soon as you can. An IT manager can definitely begin an assimilation day one if he/she so chooses. However, without a solid systems infrastructure (hardware and network) in place that has the additional capacity or the ability to increase capacity easily to accommodate the new business, the ability to manage a technology assimilation is complicated by other issues required to address infrastructure scalability. You will go much faster and smoother if you have the infrastructure foundation already in place that supports growth easily and predictably.

Strategic projects as defined here are IT projects that add significant, new capability to the business. In my acquisition assimilation example, any major technology conversion (opposed to simply continuing to maintain the existing technology) would be considered a significant change requiring a major project focus.

The real objective is not just to complete strategic projects. It should be to work on strategic projects in as productive a manner as possible so that the company can achieve the desired results with minimal problems and as cost effectively as possible.

Reacting to issues that have not been anticipated in the lower foundation levels discussed earlier when you are in the midst of a strategic project can add complexity, cause damage, and add costs that are otherwise avoidable.

VII. Key Traits of Any Successful Information Technology Manager

We have spent a good bit of time on several important concepts that are a basis of understanding before getting to this section. Now, we begin targeting key skills that are essential to be a successful IT manager, at any level. Granted, some skills are more important in certain roles than others. But, if you want to be considered by your peers and those that you work for as a well rounded manager of IT resources, pay attention to all of these skill traits.

A. Ability to Assess Needs

We spent an entire chapter on this issue to stress the importance of this skill. It is probably the most important of all the skills that follow in that without appropriate assessment, it's hard to direct IT resources in a way that meets real objectives.

Key attributes that help you assess effectively are:

- questioning techniques
- listening skills
- business experience and understanding

Developing these "interpersonal" skills is just as important as developing your technical skills. The higher you go in an organization, the more important they become. As you start reaching a CIO level, you will find that your ability to assess, prioritize, and communicate, become more important than your pure technical skills.

We have spent enough time on the importance of assessment. If you aren't comfortable with your assessment skills, find a mentor that is and work with that person to help develop your own assessment skills.

Personal Note: At IBM, one of my favorite managers always coached me and other young systems engineers to observe the other SE's and salesmen in how they conducted their business responsibilities and to add the good things to our own set of skills and leave the bad parts out.

I have taken that message to heart throughout all of my business career, and it has served me well.

B. Ability to Create a Vision

A competent manager has the ability to take his/her assessment of the situation and to develop a vision that makes sense by which to move forward. If you are at a first line manager level, the vision is much less strategic than what a CIO should be able to develop. You might also need the help of your CIO or other senior IT managers to assist you in developing a vision for your area of responsibility.

Look at it like looking at a golf score. All anyone really cares about is the score, not how you made your score. So, it doesn't matter that you might have had to ask for help as a new manager from within your company or outside of it; the bottom line is that you need to establish a short term, and then a long term vision for your responsibilities.

Sidebar: One of the messages I've always used with junior managers that worked for me is that, "If you don't decide where you want to be in "x" months and state it as an objective, you will be somewhere at that point in time but probably not where you could be or would like to be."

You have to establish a target and the vision of how you will reach your target.

As we discussed in earlier sections, a vision is more of a 20,000 to 60,000-foot level view of where you want to be and the key projects required.

<u>Personal Note:</u> *The IBM SE manager that I mentioned in an earlier example also gave me very good advice when I made the transition from an SE role to a Marketing Representative role.*

His advice was that, "You have to make a conscious choice to drop your technical expertise. In a sales role, you have to focus on sales issues and not in keeping up as technically proficient as you might like to be with all our new products. If you do, you won't be spending the necessary time to develop your sales skills and to achieve the results as a salesman that IBM needs."

That was immensely difficult for me because I went from the "top of my class", so to speak, to the "bottom of the class" overnight. It was also something that clients had difficulty with when I simply would not spend the necessary time to work through technical issues with them but forwarded their issue to another SE. Most of the difficulty for me was in the fact that I could no longer do the type of work that I really liked. Do you think this had anything to with the fact that I did not continue to sell but migrated to the technology management side?

Then why did I go into sales at IBM in the first place? I did it to better position me for management roles in the future. You see, my vision was to become a manager within IBM. Having success on both the sales and technical sides gave me additional credentials that would be of benefit later on.

It's the same reason that I majored in Accounting and Business Administration in college after leaving the Marine Corps. In the Marine Corps, I was fortunate to be placed into data processing. I learned quickly that I really enjoyed working with systems. It was also my first exposure to supervisory and management roles.

The reason that I bring the examples of why I majored in Accounting and why I went into Sales after 3 successful SE years at IBM is to make a simple point. You always should be looking to the future to insure you are positioning yourself the best way you know how to achieve a future goal. I majored in Accounting to make me more "saleable" when I finished school and it worked. In fact, that's one of the reasons that IBM expressed interest when they were looking at my credentials (a data processing background with an accounting degree).

Creating vision or setting goals is an important skill in managing technology resources effectively.

Managing is all about choosing. It's very hard to make decisions when you don't know the destination.

C. Ability to Create the Plan

Planning is key!! So many IT managers react rather than plan. Why is that?

I believe it's due to 2 reasons:

1. Planning is a skill just like anything else. Many IT managers just don't make the effort to gain this skill because they would rather spend time learning new technical expertise. It's more fun for them.

   In the example of my move to the IBM sales role, I did not develop the skills necessary to become a successful salesman – predominately because my heart was just not into it. It takes hard lessons like that at times to discover what you really like to do.

   Sidebar: *Most experienced managers know that an employee usually gravitates to the type of work and activity that he/she really likes. "Swimming upstream" in an effort to be what someone else wants you to be often has poor results. Planning is not an option for an IT manager to be successful; it is an absolute requirement.*

   If you do not have planning skills, you have to identify a way to develop them. The only way that a manager of any responsibility takes charge of his/her destiny is to establish the vision (goal) and to develop the plan that takes him there.

There are plenty of planning type classes available to learn from. In addition, two of my publications in the **IT Manager Development Series** are titled **Developing an IT Business Plan** and **Building a Strategic IT Plan**. Each has a different focus concerning IT planning, and I hope that you will take advantage of them if you need help in developing your planning skills.

Don't be like so many managers that simply do the job day to day and respond to issues that come up. Take charge and establish the plan that takes you and your organization "somewhere" rather than simply drifting to wherever the wind takes you.

2. The second reason most managers do not plan is because **planning is hard work** and takes time. This is probably the biggest reason most managers prefer to react than to plan and move forward – it's easier.

Everyone can relate to this. It's much easier to work on issues of the day and to react to what comes up than to stop what you're doing and consciously sit down to develop a detailed plan. If you have ever had to do an annual budget, you know that most people wait until the very last minute to work on the details of it. Budgeting is a form of planning! It's simply not the most important thing that you want to focus on "today"!

Have you ever heard the comment from another manager that goes like, "I'm so busy that I just don't have the time to plan."? Well, usually the reason that manager is reacting to problems all the time is because he doesn't take the time to identify ways to prevent the problems in the first place. As the company grows, the situation only becomes more difficult.

Let's see now, , , you have the skills but still don't plan effectively. The only answer to that is you had better gain the maturity and discipline to make it happen or you need to be somewhere other than in a management role. The organization you are responsible for needs your efforts to help point and move it in the right direction. If you don't want to plan, it's ok to work at something other than a management role – you might make more money and you probably will be happier.

Hold on just a minute! "Mike, that's easy for you to say because planning is easy for you and comes natural.", you might say. Actually, sitting down to develop a plan is much harder for me than implementing a project from a plan. It's the same for me as most others.

The real difference is that I realize the consequences of not planning and I have a huge desire to be successful and to do all that I can to control my (or my organization's) destiny. Without a vision and a plan, there is no way to have any control on where you will end up in your journey. Planning is like any other skill, the more you do it, the easier it becomes and the better you are at it.

Or put another way, planning is like broccoli. You know that it is good for you, but you have to eat a lot of it to acquire a taste for it.

D. Ability to Build the Team

Personal Note*: One of the hardest lessons I had to learn was as a young manager. Actually there were two lessons learned in different environments.*

The first lesson was while in the Marine Corps, I learned that you can give an order to a junior Marine and he will complete the order because he has to. But, unless his mind and heart agree with the order, he will do it with little enthusiasm or care for the quality of the work. Believe me, that was a mind-opener.

The second lesson was in my first CIO position in a very small company. My boss, the President of the company, stopped by the office one late Friday night (around 11:00 p.m.). I was working on developing some management reports that he and I had discussed the day before that we needed for the business. I was excited about the project and wanted to help the company.

He asked me where the rest of my people were and my answer was that they were probably home asleep.

The next day, he coached me on the fact that what was important in my current management role was different than in my former IBM SE role. The value that I now had with my new company was not what I could personally produce but what my entire organization could produce.

I didn't realize it then, or maybe just didn't admit it, but the fact was that I was operating at a struggling IT manager level end not the CIO level that was my title. The world is full of this today.

Thinking back about my career, both the successes and the failures, and seeing so many others struggling in their IT management roles is what triggered my desire to develop this series of publications. Success is far more achievable with just a little guidance and mentoring.

Building an effective team is a lot of fun, hard work, and requires patience. In this section, we will list the steps that I've used in the past to develop or improve many IT organizations.

1. Your assessment should have given you some conclusions regarding your IT staff as follows:
   - the skills needed
   - the experience levels needed
   - staff capacity needed
   - your gaps in skill and experience
   - areas that need additional depth
   - the processes that need to be developed
   - whether you have resources in place that can help you (i.e. senior level staff)
   - whether certain gaps or depth needs can be out-sourced
   - evaluation of the skill and experience that exists

2. Develop an organization chart that will give you a picture of the resources you need and how you need to organize to achieve success in your area of responsibility. A picture always helps me "visualize" responsibilities.

   An important note gets added here. When you are sizing up the "necessary organization", you should always know that normally you won't have a blank check from the company to just go out and hire. You have to take several elements into consideration such as:
   - Has the position been approved?
   - Is the position budgeted for?
   - Even if budgeted, is the company prepared for you to hire now?
   - Is a recruiting fee required or can you find the resource with minimal fees?
   - Are you prepared to bring a new employee into the organization?
   - Is there a job description prepared?

Other important notes that should always be in the back of your mind when hiring.

- Every new hire opportunity gives you an opportunity of adding more than just technical expertise – organizations also need:
    - maturity/leadership
    - business expertise
    - process engineers
    - planners
    - project managers
    - managers

  Anticipating future needs makes sense when you are hiring today. If you don't have future management potential on the team today, better acquire it when you hire.

- Prioritizing new hires if you have more than one position open is "key". As much as possible you want to hire in an order that addresses the following:

    - Fills critical gaps to your short term plans
    - Fills a senior position that can help you develop processes or procedures that are critical for immediate successes.
    - Adds depth to critical support areas

- You need to be ready for a new hire so prepare yourself and your organization.

Building an organization chart is important for three reasons:

1. Forces you to develop roles and responsibilities
2. Allows your staff to see how you plan to operate
3. Allows you to communicate to your client your organizational structure that is designed to support their business.

3. Prioritize the new hires. I always tended to add missing expertise before adding depth unless there was a concern of losing someone in a critical position prematurely. You have to gauge this with the dynamics of the organization.

If you're going into a situation that needs to be turned around or there are personal feelings among some of the staff that needs to be addressed, always look at the most critical positions first. You may need to hire a backup resource before you hire someone to fill a major gap.

As a manager, your radar should always be turned on. Observation skills are huge in being able to anticipate potential problems. Always build the organization that can afford to lose anyone on the team without drowning the company, including yourself.

Position your own replacement? **Absolutely!!** The first rule in management is to insure you have in place or are developing a replacement for yourself.

My management approach has always been one that empowers others to be self-sufficient. The more you can develop a staff that can run on their own, the more you position the organization (and yourself) with the opportunity to do more. Doing more for your company adds value, and adding value usually is followed by reward.

The point to all of this is to reinforce the need for you to have an overall organization resource game plan. Once you know what you need, it's much easier to start prioritizing when and how you go about hiring them.

Are you hearing a familiar theme here?

- assess
- choose the target
- prioritize
- validate
- build the plan
- execute

Don't forget the factors that must also be considered in your hiring plans like budget, preparedness, etc. Hiring just to fill positions will only get your organization to a certain point. Hiring with purpose and with an idea of anticipating future needs will take you and your organization much farther down the road to success.

4. Define the job. Even if your company does not require it, you will benefit from taking a few minutes to define the job responsibilities of the new position. This definition will clarify for the applicant as well as yourself and staff exactly what you want to achieve by this additional resource.

An IT staff member is an asset to both your organization and the company. Clearly defining how you want to use that asset is an important part of getting the results that you want. It doesn't have to be 10 pages; make it simple bullet points of what you believe key requirements are for the position.

The Internet is full of sites that can provide you with good job descriptions. Don't make the mistake of simply pulling one off the "net" and using it for your new applicant. If you must, use a generic job description and customize it for your specific position. At a minimum, put definition into the responsibilities that personalize the position to your organization and company needs. The results will be better because the focus will be greater.

5. Prepare yourself and your organization for a new hire. Why do most people dislike or resist change? I would submit to you that it's because they either are not aware that change is about to occur or they don't understand the reason for the change. Involving your staff and helping them understand your reasons and needs for a new hire and the type of individual you're looking for will help them embrace the change. It also helps the new hire fit into the organization quicker.

What does "prepare yourself" mean? It means that bringing in a new person to an organization is not "fall off the log" business. To do this effectively, you have to prepare for the new employee. You should develop a list of issues that you want to insure are covered in the first week of a new employee's time with the new company.

Spending the time to get your new asset started off on the right foot pays dividends. Don't shortcut this step.

A list of new IT employee orientation items that can be used as a starting point is listed below and in the Appendix for your use. Other than the Human Resources section, the orientation is conducted by yourself or others in the IT organization.

New Employee Orientation Guide

A. Quick tour and introductions
B. The Company
C. Mission
D. The company's business
E. Organization
F. Key departments relative to IT support
G. Strategic plans
H. Clients
  - Their needs for IT services
  - Key clients
  - The best and the worst, , ,and why
  - Key needs
  - Plans
I. Company Departments
  - Key departments and their key people
  - Department needs
  - Plans
J. Benefits Orientation and paperwork with Human Resources
  - Medical/dental insurance
  - Life insurance
  - 401k
  - W4
  - Vacation/holiday/sick day policy
  - Employee Handbook
  - Confidentiality agreement
  - Non-solicitation agreement

K. IT Organization
- Mission
- Organization chart and major focus areas
- Job description and responsibilities of the new hire
- Role within the IT organization
- Key focus areas of the new position
- Keys to success
- Overview of other key IT staff and their responsibilities
- Challenges
- Opportunities
L. IT Vision and plan for the future
M. Key projects and status
N. IT Procedures/Processes that affect the new employee
O. Performance planning and performance review guidelines
P. Career planning approach and guidelines
Q. Training guidelines
R. Miscellaneous
- Phone list
- After hours IT phone list
- Expense reporting
- Timesheets (if required)
- Security codes, cards, etc.
- User-ID & passwords to systems

In addition to the orientation, don't forget to coordinate the preparation of certain things such as:

A. Identify cube/office location
B. Phone setup
C. PC/workstation setup
D. Printer configuration setup
E. USER-ID and password setup
F. Office supplies
G. Building, facility, parking access cards
H. Business card order

Much of this goes without saying, doesn't it. The point to all of this is that the better prepared you are in helping a new employee get off to a good start the better. You will find that paying attention to a lot of these details (and others that I'm sure aren't listed) helps the employee feel welcome and positions him/her to get off to a fast start. It's well worth the effort.

Using a checklist makes it a simple task every time you add a new employee.

E. Ability to Focus the Resources

Many organizations have a focus challenge. I can't tell you how many times I've seen an organization that has people running all over the place trying to get things done. They are certainly working hard, but their effective output is marginal due to a lack of focus.

Once you have focused the overall organization on a goal or vision, you have to drop down to the next level to insure each person in the organization is focused on his/her set of responsibilities that will get you there.

Sidebar: *Let's use an example. Imagine your team is an offensive line of a football team. The defense wants to "sack the quarterback" and will do all in their power to do so. Each member of your offensive line has a responsibility to "block out" certain areas of the line. If a defensive lineman moves around, the offense still focuses on blocking "zones" or "areas", and does not run around trying to block an individual defensive player wherever he might move to.*

Technology organizations need to look at it the same way. Sure, you may have a utility resource that can do everything but as your company grows, it becomes more necessary to specialize.

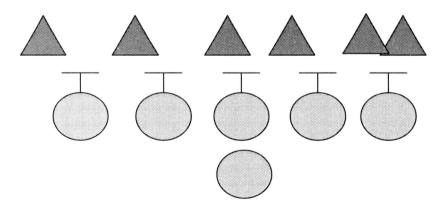

The right side of the line can't worry about the left side. They need to know that the skills and focus on the left side will accomplish their mission so that the "team" succeeds.

The same scenario holds true for an IT organization. Put yourself into a CIO position. During the assessments, the CIO identified the issues of the IT organization and the capabilities of his staff. Developing an organization plan that has appropriate focus on different components of the IT challenge is important in the same way that a coach puts his offensive line together to defend against an expected defense.

IT support challenges might include:
- business applications development
- business applications support
- implementing new infrastructure services and architecture
- support desk
- documentation
- software installation teams
- research and development
- data center requirements
- systems uptime requirements
- training
- establishing standards
- establishing workable service level agreements
- and many more

It's important for the CIO to develop an organization structure that can meet all the critical needs efficiently to help the company move forward. In order to do that, the CIO must have a clear picture of what must be "blocked" and which resources will "block" specific issues.

Getting the staff to stay focused to their designated zone is another challenge.

How does a manager motivate his employees to stay focused on their assigned area? Employees focus on the areas that lead to reward. We all do. That's a good thing.

The best way to help the employee focus to a given set of responsibilities (or zone) is to:

1. Define the job requirement. That's done in two ways. First, provide a job description that helps identify the position. Secondly, and more important is to develop a Performance Plan that spells out what you want your employee to achieve and hold him accountable to it.

   A good Performance Plan is used as a tool and not something to use against an employee. Good performance planning cannot only help your employees stay focused; it can help enhance their performance output.

2. Communicate your vision and reinforce each person's role in achieving it.

Often!!

I discuss the details of developing and implementing effective Performance Plans in the publication titled **Building a Successful IT Organization**. Performance planning and reviews are essential ingredients in obtaining success from your organization.

Often, managers view performance planning as a burden required by Human Resources. It really should not be looked at that way. If you want to maximize the output of your employee and you want to help develop the employee's skills and value to the company, look at performance planning and reviews as the greatest tools you have to do so.

Performance planning and review sessions can be some of the most enjoyable part of managing employees, , , even those required to address improvements needed. That's what management is all about – not what you can do but how much you can accomplish through your team.

Watching an empowered, motivated team perform is an awesome thing. Every team has the potential to achieve great things; most do not. Managers make the difference.

F. Ability to Implement a Client Service 'Mindset'

Just because an organization says they have a "client service approach" does not make it so. Your assessments should have indicated as to whether the IT organization you have responsibility for is really delivering IT services and support with a client service "mindset". If you don't know, better read the chapter on assessment again.

What is a client service "mindset"?

Glad you asked. In my approach, it has more to do with how IT approaches the support of its clients than in what it does.

First, a key point. The client is always right, , , but the client may not be "correct" or "accurate". What I mean by this is that the client is paying for your support. Yes, even if your IT client is another department or employee within your company (an internal client), they are essentially paying for your organization's existence. With that said, the client has every right to disagree with or to be unhappy with your services, , , to a point.

What I am not saying is that you should do everything the client says and do it with the biggest smile ever seen by mankind. It's the IT organization's responsibility to provide leadership to its clients as it relates to technology issues. After all, they really are buying that along with the specific products and services that you provide.

If the client is unhappy, it's up to the manager to help establish an appropriate satisfaction level. Remember the emphasis on assessment? You never get away from the necessity to develop clear assessments of situations. Client problems are no different. Understanding the issues surrounding a dissatisfied client has opportunity written all over it.

THE
SILVER
LINING
IN EVERY
CLOUD

Let's list items that constitute a client service "mindset":

- Priorities are driven by the client's needs
- The client participates in establishing priorities
- The client is not surprised by changes implemented by IT
- The client's system availability is always taken into consideration when implementing new technology
- IT has escalation processes in place to minimize system downtime
- IT communicates to the client frequently and proactively in troubleshooting problems
- IT managers proactively manage client expectations in a manner that allows the IT organization to meet or exceed expectations
- IT managers step up to inappropriate client issues or behavior that affects the support of their systems
- The client is involved in the quality assurance of new technology releases and partners with IT rather than simply receiving technology services from IT
- Follow-up is automatic. When an IT employee tells the client they will do something, you can "take it to the bank" that it gets done or someone communicates to the client the reasons it can't be done before the client has to call and ask.

Let's talk about follow-up. This is such a **BIG** issue!!! It is also a very basic issue that is vital to positive client service. You can have the best technology resources and the best implementation project plans in the world and have a totally unsuccessful IT organization if it does not follow-up well. On the other hand, you can have less capable people and be considered an excellent IT organization when you communicate and follow up exceptionally well. I'll take the second type of organization any day.

There really is no excuse for not following up!

That's not to say that you don't have to deliver; you do. The client wants more from IT, but they want it predictably and in an informed, no surprises, way. Your ability to develop within your organization excellent follow-up skills positions the organization to be able to make mistakes without getting slammed by your client. Poor follow-up skills and making mistakes gets you a lot of scars so emphasize to your group the necessity of following up and communicating well.

Reward those attributes and watch how motivated your organization becomes.

Obviously, there is a lot of balancing required. If you have 100 clients, every client cannot drive every priority that IT has. You can, however, assemble a small, representative user group steering committee that's empowered to speak for all users in developing priorities with the IT organization.

It's important to know that the client has a strong need to feel that the IT organization is an advocate in doing all that it can to understand his issues and needs, to be able to relate those issues to technical solutions where possible, and to work on the issues that are important to his business.

If your organization operates in such a manner and has a great smile at the same time, watch out! You're headed for success.

Most of managing a client so that you maintain an excellent client relationship is based upon your organization's client service skills. The client looks to the IT manager for a path to the "promised land". He does not expect you to have the solution off the top of your head. I've never seen a client refuse to give the manager time to develop an appropriate plan to solve the problems he was experiencing.
In fact, as mentioned in an earlier example, the client will often pay more to arrive at a workable solution. When they balk, it's

usually because there is no confidence you will deliver. You can't fix "past sins", but you can establish rapport with the client and usually work out a solution that resolves the issue. When you do, **<u>you must</u>** put steps in place that guarantees that you will accomplish what you say you will do.

Never build a plan that has a lot of risk or that "you hope works" in a problem client situation. You're just setting yourself up. Be practical, logical, and build some room for mistakes. Also, put the resources on critical parts of the plan that you can trust will get their part done very well. You'll be glad you did.

G. Ability to Manage Projects

Depending upon your level within the IT organization, you may not have to be that close to actually managing projects. However, regardless of your position it's important for you to understand the importance of effective project management and be able to reinforce the use of project management disciplines within your organization.

A project of any real size and complexity has a much higher potential for success when it is clearly defined, communicated, and followed. In this section, we will talk through some basics of project management to pay attention to. A more detailed description with supporting tools is included in the publication titled appropriately **IT Project Management**. For more information, take a look at the Table of Contents at www. mde.net/cio .

If you are genuinely interested in developing project management skills for yourself or within your organization, there is a certification titled PMP (Project Management Professional) available through the Project Management Institute (PMI). Many companies provide formal training that can assist your efforts.

One such company is PMSI-Project Mentors, (a Provant company) based in Atlanta, Georgia. PMSI specializes in managing projects of all sizes and complexities for other companies and they have their own training organization that can assist a company in developing whatever level of project management skill that is needed. Their company web site is at www.pmsinc.com . They have an excellent track record of managing projects that are completed on time and within budget.

On time & within budget!

These words are music to any senior level executive at any company you will find. Are you aware that more than 70% of all large projects that IT organizations undertake either do not get completed on time or completed within budget, , , or both? It is a huge cost impact to companies everywhere.

In this document I don't push, or even encourage you to acquire PMP credentials. The encouragement that I want to give you is that every time your area of responsibility has a project to complete of any significance, you should use sound project management techniques that help insure you complete the project successfully.

Remember, we talked about finding yourself in some unknown destination if you don't first identify your destination objective. That was the vision part. The project plan lays out "how you will get to your destination". Many IT managers try to get by without developing formal project plans. It's another example that it takes work to develop a project plan and to use it as you implement your project. Taking shortcuts usually has the project ending up "in the ditch" by either missing the dates, exceeding the budget, or both.

Before I leave the project management credentials discussion, let me say this. PMP credentials are becoming more and more of a standard in the project manager circles. More companies are becoming aware of the need for solid project management expertise to improve the predictability and cost effectiveness of getting projects completed. If you plan to become a professional project manager as a career, you should pursue getting your PMP. It will open doors for you in the long run that might not be open otherwise.

Let's discuss briefly the major components of managing a project.

Project Management Components

1. Initiating the Project
2. Planning the Project
3. Project Execution
4. Controlling the Project
5. Project Completion

Simple so far, right? Managing projects effectively does not have to be overly complex. Sure, there may be complex issues or decisions that have to be made within the project, but managing a project can actually be very straightforward.

Let's take each component and break it down a bit. We don't go into great detail in this publication as I dedicate an entire publication titled **IT Project Management** in **the IT Manager Development Series**.

1. Initiating the Project

Initiating the project requires you to establish a few assumptions before you begin the plan such as:

- project goal and objectives
- preliminary timelines
- preliminary budget
- estimate of staff requirements
- communication methods to use

As you work through the project needs and the estimates of resources (staff and dollars) needed, the output should be a Project Charter document that defines what the project is, how it will be completed (at a high level), an estimate of the cost and time to complete the project, and the deliverables of the project. The Project Charter is essentially the vehicle used to gain concurrence from the business owners that the project objectives, approach, and deliverables are appropriate and acceptable.

You should not go forward without an agreement from the stakeholders that you have defined the requirements of the project accurately. To do so puts you into a very vulnerable position and makes it extremely difficult to achieve success in the project.

2. Planning the Project

Once the Project Charter is agreed upon, it's time to build the detailed project plan. In it's simplest form, the plan defines the specifics of the project as follows:

- project scope
- resources required (staff)
- budget required and how it will be spent
- the plan
    - tasks
    - responsibilities
    - completion
    - dependencies of tasks on other task completions
- communication plans (status meetings, etc.)
- risks

Depending upon the project, this part can be very extensive to very basic. I have run very large systems conversion projects on simple spreadsheets and used e-mail to provide much of the communication.

The real issue is there needs to be a formal plan that spells out what, when, and by whom the tasks will be accomplished. You will find as I have that if you take the time to develop the detailed plan, modify it as you need to, hold regular status sessions to review and understand progress, then things usually move along smoothly.

It's simply amazing that when a person goes into a project status meeting with peers and the project manager, most do not want to be seen as the weak link or the part that's holding the project up. Peer pressure is a powerful and wonderful thing.

As you develop your project plan, keep two things in mind:

1. There will be surprises.
2. You have to have "buffer" in the plan. The larger the plan, the more buffer you potentially need.

I'm convinced that the main reasons most projects are not completed on time is that plans are not developed in the first place and secondly, most plans do not anticipate problems to occur and have no "safety valve".

It's the same as budgeting for an organization. I have never missed hitting my budget for the year. All you have to do is to put appropriate buffers in the most prevalent places that you might have a budgetary surprise. If you anticipate things that can go wrong and plan accordingly, you're covered.

No one likes the manager that is always falling short because he/she did not plan for surprises. The bottom line is that you miss your plan or budget. NOT GOOD!!

Everyone likes the manager that meets or exceeds his plan or budget. You want to work with those that you can count on. Building buffers that anticipate likely problems is an appropriate and a smart thing to do. Failing to have contingencies is like planning to fail!

One of the sayings that I'm fond of is.

" Anticipate what you don't expect!"

What in the world does this mean????

It simply means, "think about what can go wrong, and build into your plan or budget some portion that handles the unexpected". Anticipating, planning, and asking "what if" are good exercises to spend time on occasionally as you develop your detailed plans.

Things can go wrong and will go wrong so don't put yourself into the position that to have a successful project everything has to work like clockwork. It rarely happens.

3. Project Execution

As you begin execution of the plan, you should begin sizing up early on as to whether your project scope appears to be appropriate and that the right resources were defined, available, and capable of executing the plan.

Project execution means the project manager is constantly evaluating the dynamics of the project and the parts that affect the final outcome such as the resource, definition of the scope, budget, etc. Every week should provide the project manager with more insight as to how accurate the detailed project plan is.

We should emphasize that a project plan is dynamic and not static. As you develop a project plan at the beginning of the project, there will be issues that you simply will not be aware of that can make the project easier to achieve or harder to complete. A good project manager must develop the skill to know when it is appropriate to modify the schedule or the budget. Remember what I said about building in "buffers"?

As you are executing the project, you cannot over emphasize the need for communication. You should do all that you can to over communicate to everyone who is part of the project. It's important for the "right hand to know what the left hand is doing" and vice versa.

Communicating with the project team weekly eliminates opportunities for the project to get off track. Any major problem issue tends to be identified early and gives you and the team the time to address it before it becomes such a major issue that it throws off the entire project.

4. Controlling the Project

Controlling the project means the project manager is monitoring the key issues of the project so that the project is completed on time and on budget. This usually means tracking the costs as expenses are incurred and monitoring the completion of tasks as they are completed. A good project manager is always looking forward and doing the things today that help facilitate the issues and task completions that are required weeks ahead.

Taking corrective action to keep the project tracking or changing components of the project to support the ultimate goal are responsibilities of the project manager. Unless the project manager has a process in place that organizes the project and tracks expenses, it's difficult to know that a project is getting 'off track'. Controlling skills require good organization, monitoring, and communication skills.

Planning and anticipating – the two biggest words in project management. Do these well along with monitoring and communicating well and you will have success after success.

5. Project Completion

At the completion of a project you should provide your client with a Completed Project Report. This report should revisit the deliverables and provide the client with information describing the completion of the project, the cost, and any exception issues that are unresolved. At the presentation of the report, the project typically comes to a close.

Depending upon the company environment you are working in, the use of project management tools will be different. A professional organization where many or most users are familiar with a tool such as Microsoft Project is actually the minority of companies out there today. Most technical managers and departments or clients do not use and are not familiar with this software.

If you are lucky enough to be a part of a company that uses these tools, then you should take advantage of them. They are very good and can be extremely valuable, especially for very large, complex projects.

In most cases, I have found that another approach using Microsoft EXCEL or Microsoft WORD can be just as effective. In addition, most users have and are familiar with these two products. It still gets down to the fact that if the plan is developed and documented, and you conduct status meetings in such a way that holds the team accountable, then any tool can be effective. It simply boils down to whether you are disciplined and want to work for the positive results that you will achieve.

Much more information on effective project management and a few tools that I have developed to manage projects is included in the publication titled **IT Project Management** and in the **IT Manager toolKit.**.

H. Ability to Implement Change Management Processes

Being a manager of IT resources means you will have to deal with constant change. In fact, an example provided in an earlier graphic shows you just how much outside elements affect the world of an IT manager. Each of these "influencers" create issues that cause change to occur within an IT organization. And, oh by the way, this is just a list of a few of the outside influences that affects the IT manager's day to day work environment.

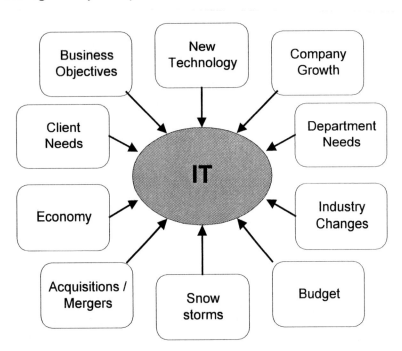

Does it appear to you that the outside "influencers" all have "arrows" pointing to the IT department? Well, it should. In many ways, the arrows are flying all the time looking for a place to land. There are times in any IT professional's career that he feels like he has a 'target' on his back.

Why do you think I have "Snow Storm" listed? Very simple. Snow storms and other natural catastrophe situations such as flood, hurricanes, earthquakes, etc. all impact and cause change to take place in an IT manager's business of keeping his systems stable and operational.

Even if your IT organization is not making significant changes to its technology, the fact remains that change is occurring every day for one reason or another. Therefore, you must have a change management process in place that works.

Industry changes that impact a company that deals with software regulatory changes, say from the IRS or other government agency, can potentially catch you off guard and have significant adverse impact to the business until the change is addressed. Try collecting for Medicare healthcare services when you don't have their latest regulatory changes in place. Your cash flow can suddenly stop.

An IT manager needs to have a couple of things going when we discuss "ability to implement change management processes".

First, the manager has to have an early warning system in place that helps him know about upcoming changes relevant to his responsible area as early as possible. The CEO doesn't really care about the excuse you might have if cash flow dries up.

Be prepared!!

Second, the manager should establish appropriate procedures to handle changes including:

1. Logging and tracking change requests
2. Justifying changes to be completed
3. Prioritizing projects and work requests
4. Communicating project priorities and work status
5. Project development procedures
6. Quality Assurance process
7. Implementation procedures
8. Recovery procedures
9. Escalation procedures

Let's discuss each of the areas of a good change management process. You can put this list into context of most any IT job. It applies to programming changes for software applications. It applies to managing an infrastructure team responsible for supporting systems or teams that implement new services. It applies to the computer center. It applies to a support desk.

1. Logging and tracking change requests

I have always approached this issue simply. Develop a Change Request Form first and train your users to use it. Sample Change Request forms that I've used in the past along with a sample Backlog Request Log are shown and discussed below. There are also blank copies in Appendix D.

Approaching something simply does not mean "casually". One of the greatest challenges you have as an IT manager is being able to manage your "customer's" expectations. Unless you have a process that clearly identifies what the priorities are and what your organization is working on, lots of luck.

Failing to communicate with your user regularly on these issues does one thing – let's you keep track for yourself but it does nothing to manage your client's expectations.

I have always considered managing infrastructure issues as somewhat of a different discipline than managing changes to business applications (programming development and support). For this reason, I have always used different forms and logs to manage the change management processes for these two disciplines.

Before we get into the processes that I've developed for my own organizations over the years, we should discuss the use of tools that can help you in this regard first. There are software tools available to log and track change requests. You can even build an online change request application for your company intranet. I've used all of these approaches and they all work fine.

For the purpose of this publication, we will use simple Microsoft WORD and EXCEL files to discuss maintaining a change request input and log system. They will work very well. You can also set up the field definitions used in these documents into a Microsoft ACCESS, or other database, and take historical reporting to a much greater level if you want.

Many of you reading this will already be well ahead of me and that's perfectly all right. Our purpose here is to illustrate the key parts of what you want to track, why, and how.

What's the purpose of initiating a more formal process of taking change requests and then keeping track of them? The ultimate objective will be to measure your performance improvement. Initially, it will be used to create a system that lets you, the manager, determine what the workload really is and to establish a level of performance you are actually delivering.

Have you ever heard a technical resource tell everyone that he/she is not working hard? Usually, you don't hear this. More than likely you hear, "I can't get everything done because there is so much to do and not enough resources." The reality of what a tracking system can show might be such that "overworked" is exactly the issue. On the other hand, it might show that there is plenty of capacity but your resources are spending a lot of time on issues that are not very important.

Wouldn't it be great to know one way or the other?

Whatever you find, having the data that tells you what the issues are, who is taking care of those issues, and how long it's taking to resolve them is an invaluable tool for a manager at any level.

"He who has the data has the power!!"

Let's take infrastructure (systems, networks, desktops, and peripheral devices) first. The following form is an **Infrastructure Change Request Form** that I have used when there was no help desk process in place to manage the capture of incoming requests and keeping track of them.

What does a Change Request Form accomplish?

First and foremost it establishes a managed method of initiating a request to IT as opposed to the "hallway request".

Secondly, the form requires a manager or responsible level supervisor to initiate the request to IT. With the request comes the appropriate authority and justifycation for IT to work on the request.

Third, it gives IT a document trail.

Fourth, it has pertinent data fields included so that supporting information needed by IT can be provided. Helps streamline the process.

Fifth, when the request is logged it gives the manager the ability to quickly see the backlog of all requests, who has been assigned the task, and how long it's been on the request list.

Lastly, when the requests are logged and tracked through completion, historical reporting of your support activity is available. If you want to improve the support capability of your IT environment, you need to understand your business.

Having the data can help you become aware of trends, key requestors, productivity of your staff, and overall responsiveness of your organization. It also gives you an opportunity of establishing a baseline of your support performance level by identifying key indicators and monitoring progress each month, quarter, or yearly.

Wouldn't it be great to be able to quantify for your client and your company the improvements you are making in your IT support organization? Wouldn't it be great to know whether you are improving or not for yourself, and if so, by some quantifiable measurements? It all starts with the Change Request form.

IT Infrastructure Change Request Form

Employee Equipment Change request

____ Add   Requested by: _____
____ Change   Request Date: _____
____ Delete

Employee Name: _____
Department: _____
Effective Date: _____
Physical Location: _____
                   _____

Equipment Needed:

____ PC
____ Laptop Computer
____ New Phone
____ Special phone needs ?
_____
_____
____ Fax
____ External modem line

Software Needs:

____ MS/Office (Includedw/PC)
____ FRX
Other software needs:
_____
_____
_____

Services Needed:

____ AS/400 (Billing,A/R)
____ CA
____ NC,SC
____ New Jersey
____ Indiana
____ Ohio
____ Texas

____ AS/400 Infinium (Acct.)
____ FRX

Primary Printer _____

Other services needed:
_____
_____
_____

Submit form to Information Technology Support Desk for completion:

119

The form that is shown is obviously two things. It is simple which it needs to be. It was also developed for a specific company use as can be seen by some of the fields represented on the form.

For a larger company you may want to include justification and approval fields. In the environment that I used this particular form it wasn't really necessary. You should customize the form, whether it's paper or an online form, to meet the needs you want to address. After all, it's your business to take responsibility for.

2. Justifying changes to be completed

Your IT department can't be in the business of responding to everything someone might want. It all has to be managed. Even though the requestor might really want or need something, the company can't afford for IT to fulfill any and all requests.

Establishing standards, especially for desktop PC's, peripherals, and software are very important in creating both a stable infrastructure environment and one that can be very supportable.

The same is true for business application programming requests. Programming managers have two responsibilities that must be balanced – cost effective solutions and high levels of client service. These two issues do not always compliment one another. They can actually conflict. That's why I use the word "balance".

One means of balancing user or client requests is to require management review and approval as well as cost justification for all programming changes or enhancements. You can reinforce standards, appropriate business reasons for requests, etc. with managers that have the authority to approve the requests. In large organizations, you have to work through the management team as opposed to trying to reinforce these issues with the entire company staff.

Another real reason for requiring management approval of programming requests is that often people in the same organization are not aware of projects being worked on for their counterparts in another area of the building or another city. By requiring requests to be reviewed and approved at the appropriate department management level, you insure that there will be less of a chance for duplication of working on conflicting items.

Programming Change Request Form

Information Technology
Programming Request   No. _____

Requested By: _____ Dept. _____

Request Date: _____ Priority Request _____ (High, Med, Low)

Supervisor Approval: _____ Date: _____

<u>Description of Problem / Issue:</u> (Attach supporting documentation as needed)

_____

_____

_____

_____

_____

_____

_____

<u>Justification:</u>

Savings / Benefits (Be specific as possible): _____

_____

_____

_____

<u>IT Department Use Only</u>

Est. Programming hours _____ Comments : _____

Est. Benefit $ value _____ _____

Est. Programming cost _____ _____

_____

_____

122

With this form you will see a cost justification section. I have learned over many years of managing programming resources that most requests submitted will add very little real value to the company's bottom line.

Unless there is a conscious effort of the management team to reinforce the concept of using the company's resources (in this case programmers) cost effectively, you will find your programmers working a great deal on those "nice to have" items rather than the projects that improve the company's position.

There are many reasons as to why clients and users often submit requests that have little or no value:

- do not understand the need to focus on tangible issues
- do not appreciate the cost of programming resources (in other words there is a cost in delivering any programming change)
- emotional "wants" versus critical needs
- justification isn't required

You will also notice that this form is very simple as well. The purpose of the form is to capture the highlights of a change (supporting documentation will often be attached) so that IT can log the request and add it to the list of items that need to be reviewed for prioritization and work assignment.

3. Prioritizing projects and work requests

Did you say "prioritize"? There is that word again!!!

Some clients have the greatest difficulty with this concept. Prioritizing the work has as much to do with your success as an IT manager as other management skills. No IT organization can work on every issue that comes up at once. Failing to prioritize will certainly spell doom sooner or later.

How do you prioritize?

You should involve your primary clients that are giving you the requests. It develops more of a partnership and has them involved in achieving their desired results. Plus, the IT department is not necessarily in the best seat to make the determination of which project is most important.

Prioritizing programming projects must take several factors into consideration including need, reasons for the change, implications of making and not making the change, cost, resource effort, status of other projects, resource expertise availability, etc.

It's usually harder to decide what you don't work on than it is to decide what to work on. Just remember that a key to delivering IT services viewed as consistent with company needs has a lot to do with requiring your client to help you prioritize your projects. To do that you have to help the client understand your capacity for getting things done and that doing it right the first time saves time and money.

A general rule of thumb that you can use to help you prioritize requests would be to look at each priority in the following rank of importance:

- A. Affects cash flow
- B. Business compliance
- C. Client retention
- D. Increases revenue
- E. Increases productivity
- F. Enhances client satisfaction

As you see, the first three have to do with current business operation needs – maintaining cash flow, keeping your clients and staying in business. The next two items are issues that improve the business, and the last includes items that make the client/user feel better but may not do very much for the business.

The 'meat and potatoes' of managing programming priorities are in the first 4 areas so make them your priorities as you look at each request.

Another way to help your client or user better understand the need to help prioritize a programming backlog is to put an hourly programming rate on each project. If two projects are estimates of 100 hours each and the client knows that the cost is $50 per hour (use whatever number you want), then he can get to a decision quickly as to which project he wants to pay $5,000 for.

Internal clients, especially, don't look at the true cost of your programming projects. Help them understand it and they will help you prioritize appropriately.

When you work on your client's true priorities you are well on your way toward a great client relationship. A tool that helps you and your client to prioritize the backlog of requests is to maintain a **Backlog Report**. Tools are readily available to log and maintain backlog requests, assign them to IT resources, etc. You can also develop one in Microsoft Access with minimal effort.

For this exercise, I'll use an EXCEL spreadsheet sample that can work for you as well.

Having a Backlog Report gives you a quick visual on how much there is to do, or at least how much has been requested. It can also tell you where the requests are coming from. It can do a lot for you if you set it up right; and, it doesn't take a lot of effort.

IT Project Backlog

(Date)

PROJECT	PRI	Req. By	Expected Start	Expected End	Assigned Prog. Resource	Est. Hours	Comments
4. Prjecd # 4	M	Dept-A	5/1/01	6/1/01	Ray	30	
6. Prjecd # 6	L	Dept-B	5/1/01	6/1/01	Ray	10	
10. Prjecd # 6	H	Dept-A	3/20/01	6/1/01	Bob	150	
11. Prjecd # 11	H	Dept-A	3/29/01	6/15/01	Ken	100	
28. Prjecd # 28	M	Client1	5/31/01	6/30/01	Ray	20	

The *Projects* included are only the projects that have not yet been completed. You may have a project on the list for a year or more. If it never becomes a priority it will stay unless you reach an agreement with the requestor to eliminate it.

The *Priority* is Low, Medium, or High. To highlight the high priorities you can shade the appropriate blocks. One assumption that you may have to work on is that it would seem obvious that your programmers should work on the *High* priorities first. Not necessarily.

Because you may have multiple clients providing requests, they won't all have the same priority. Developing measures to manage the prioritization activities to fit your programming capacity can be a challenge but achievable. If you have to, form a user committee that reviews the backlog and assigns priorities with you that fits within your programming capacity.

Requested by is the department requesting the change.

Expected start and *end dates* are added when the project is actually assigned to a programmer and a finished estimate date is put in to target when you expect the project to be placed into production.

Adding the *Assigned Programming Resource* column lets you see what your programmers are working on. It also is a good reference for looking at assigned projects when you begin tracking the quality of your programming releases (more on that later).

Estimated Hours lets you see how the projects are assigned and relative balance among your programming staff. In the past I have even used a total actual hours column to compare the actual time of effort compared to the estimate to improve our ability to forecast work efforts.

When the user can look at the outstanding list of backlog items and estimated hours that his department has requested, it makes it easier for to prioritize. Anything you can do that helps you make it easier for the client and gives you awareness of your business is a good thing to do.

My management approach has always been to use reports like this to conduct weekly or monthly status meetings with the IT staff and to host prioritization meetings with clients.

EXCEL has certain limitations obviously, but it's a quick startup if nothing is available and each column can be sorted quickly to allow review of the dynamics of your programming organization. It's also easy enough to transfer completed projects to another spreadsheet for basic historical reporting.

I'm a strong proponent that you don't really need the software tool that provides you every feature you can think of. In reality, you will probably only use a few key features to manage your business very effectively.

4. Communicating project priorities and work status

Getting the priorities defined is one thing. You must also communicate them to the client and your staff as well as other company areas that need to know. It's very important to communicate where you're headed. Don't forget this.

"What we have, , , is a failure to communicate."
(Quote from the movie, Cool Hand Luke)

Well, yes, you're right. The context of the phrase in the movie doesn't have anything to do with this section, but I like the quote and it's a test to see if you are still awake, so I used it.

Failing to communicate your priorities allows the client to make their own guess as to where they think you're headed, and guess what! Their guess will rarely line up with your plan so the odds of being successful are rarer than finding four leaf clovers.

Remember earlier when I commented that much, if not most, of your success in managing IT resources is based on the softer, people skills as opposed to the technical skills. Communicating effectively is one of the examples.

5. Project development procedures

In order to deliver programming changes effectively, you have to have standards and procedures in place that allow the organization to deliver predictably and consistently. The same holds true in completing infrastructure projects.

In my experience, these procedures include:

    A. Designing the project with details of deliverables
    B. Gaining agreement from the requestor
    C. Incorporating development standards (programming, desktop, etc.)
    D. Incorporating project management standards
    E. Internal testing (both the developer and an internal QA resource)

6. Quality Assurance process that gets the requestor involved early

The best insurance you can have for developing procedures that help you implement changes predictably, especially programming, is to include the client in your testing and quality assurance procedures. When they have a vested part of insuring that it's right, you have a real partnership as well as testing insight that you just can't get from your IT staff.

For large projects, develop a test plan that helps guide the client in how to test and key areas that really need the attention. Establish sign-off criteria to provide both yourself and the client knowledge that critical parts have been reviewed sufficiently.

7. Implementation procedures

Putting enhancements into production requires care and caution. Dotting the "i's" and crossing the "t's" is essential at this stage. All the best laid plans can be for naught if this step is handled sloppily.

Implementation procedures should be developed for each function within IT that implements changes. Implementing programming changes should be done in a way to minimize user interruption. Steps should be developed that forces the resource charged with the implementation part to take every step required to implement the changes successfully. Develop a checklist and use it.

Communication of the changes to be implemented should be delivered to affected users prior to implementing the changes. Users hate to be surprised, don't you?

Systems architecture or other documentation maintained on your systems should be updated appropriately. User documentation should also be updated as part of the implementation release.

8. Recovery procedures

Managing an IT organization in a dynamic environment that requires lots of change pleads for you to have sound recovery procedures. Regardless of your responsibility in IT, it makes a lot of sense for you to confirm for yourself that IT has sound backup and recovery procedures in place.

There will also be times when you need to go back to that data purge that everyone agreed had to take place but amazingly a year later the need arises to get to something imbedded in the archived (we hope it is) data.

As you implement change, evaluate "what if" scenarios that are unsuccessful and determine options that you have to recover. By playing "devil's advocate", you will be anticipating the unexpected and will be better prepared to pull it back into place.

9. Escalation procedures

Just as you need sound recovery procedures, you should also put into place escalation procedures to handle potential problems that might arise. Enhancing your systems goes a long way. Positioning yourself to respond quickly in the event of a problem establishes true professionalism that helps you stand above the rest.

Personal Note: *In the middle of a system migration that was to be followed by another in 30 days, I delayed the second implementation for another 30 days after the first 'cut-over'. The reason was to insure that we had sufficient resource available to focus on potential problems that might be uncovered after "go-live" rather than having them focus on the next project too quickly.*

If the conversion went without issue, a 30-day lag was more than sufficient. The problem was that a 30-day lag placed too much pressure on the success of both projects if anything unexpected came up.

Remember Murphy's Law, "What can go wrong will go wrong." Build buffer into your plans and you will achieve more success.

I. Ability to Lead and Motivate

In the Marine Corps I learned the value of leading versus ordering. People are hungry for leadership, especially IT resources. Most people in IT want to be helpful, want to add value, and want to be respected for their contribution. Provide leadership that provides positive responses to those needs and they will go to any length to support you.

Ignore them and be ignored.

This is a very important topic. So much so that I commit two entire publications in my **IT Manager Development Series** to this area. One is titled **Building a Successful IT Organization**. The second is **IT Staff Motivation and Development**.

Understanding that as a manager it matters little in what you personally can do is the first step. What matters the most is the ability your team has to accomplish things. As the IT manager you are the quarterback of your team. I've never seen a great quarterback win very much without good players playing their positions well.

You are the catalyst and the motivator. The team responds to your actions, both good and bad. They are also always watching for your lead. Your example is extremely important and the manner in which you conduct yourself will be felt and repeated by your team.

Leaders can be developed. I'm a perfect example. My successes have not been because I'm a natural leader. They have been developed because I care and I have watched how others achieve success in leadership roles.

Most of my leadership and management approaches are not original; they are a combination of a lot of experiences that I have observed that work.

Align yourself with the positive forces of your company and watch the successful managers for traits that you can incorporate into your own management style.

I'll give you a few tips that I believe are important leadership traits.

1. Treat people with respect.
2. Encourage "team". I have a favorite saying, "We will all succeed as a team; no one succeeds individually unless the team succeeds."
3. Support your team in difficult situations. Deal with tough clients.
4. Always strive to do 'the right thing' more than 'doing things right'.
5. Hire good people.
6. Address poor performance and achieve appropriate levels of performance or terminate the resource.
7. Always provide your team with the necessary tools.
8. Communicate your organization vision.
9. Communicate project status regularly with all involved or impacted.
10. Coach individual performance behind closed doors.
11. Find a way to compliment every individual (where possible) in staff meetings,
12. Hold frequent staff meetings and cover company news as well as today's business issues.
13. Reward the behavior and achievements that you want.
14. Promote your team to senior management.
15. Track results and communicate achievements as well as failures.
16. Take the time to explain the reasons behind change within the company.
17. Ask them, "How was your weekend?", , , and mean it.
18. Persuade versus order. (this was hard for a young Marine to learn)
19. Empower individuals to take on more responsibility, but stay close enough to support them so that they

succeed. Mistakes are OK, but don't damage a young asset by letting them fail in a critical situation.

20. Be positive and promote the opportunities of your company.
21. Develop plans with your staff involved.
22. Ask for their opinion. They usually have great ideas and insight.
23. Pay attention to performance reviews and salary reviews.
24. Help them identify what they want and direct their efforts to achieve their goals. This means developing appropriate goals.
25. Have an 'open door' policy. Nothing is more important than working through an individual's challenges. Saying you have an 'open door' policy doesn't mean you work that way. The staff member has to feel comfortable that he/she can bring a problem to your attention without recourse. Don't shoot the messenger.
26. Buy pizza or have an ice cream party and have some fun. Motivated people perform better and it costs next to nothing.
27. As the manager, always take the responsibility for your organization's failures. Never blame the staff to your client.
28. Say 'thank you'.

There are many more leadership tips as you would expect, but taking the opportunity to implement this list into your management style will create a positive following of your staff.

You are given a position or a title; you **earn** respect. What's more, you constantly have to earn respect. People follow leaders and those they respect, not titles or people of position. Just as in the Marine Corps, my staff would obey the order, , , sometimes halfheartedly, , , they charge the hill for a leader. When you see it working, it is one of the most powerful things you can experience as a manager.

J. Ability to Communicate Effectively

An IT manager must be able to communicate in four directions:

Senior
Management

Peers

Clients

Employees

1. to the staff
2. to peers (other managers)
3. to the client
4. to senior management

Communication approach is different for all four groups. There are details and issues that you must discuss with the staff very openly that you don't necessarily need to concern a client with. Senior managers don't tend to need as much detail as for you to net out goals, plans, issues, and risks.

Developing communication skills to be effective in all four areas is important, especially as your management responsibilities expand. A CIO that has to address the Board of Directors may only have a 20-minute segment. You don't get into a lot of detail in 20 minutes, nor should you. They just want to know what you're going to do, the major benefits, and a sense that it's achievable with manageable risk.

If you are not comfortable with public speaking, take a class and seek out opportunities to stand in front of people to develop speaking skills. If you want to become an IT manager that is viewed as a leader, you have to be able to articulate your plans and issues in front of a group, possibly a large group.

Personal Note: *In my second week at IBM, I went to Atlanta for my first training class. Fresh out of college at 27 years old because of my Marine Corps tour, I was what you would consider a more mature college hire than the normal 21-23 year old.*

The first day's assignment for Day-2 was for each of us to develop a flip chart presentation of a specific topic we were assigned and to deliver a stand-up presentation to the group the next day. It would be filmed and graded.

Well, I developed an excellent set of flip charts; my organization and graphic skills are ok. Late that night I began to think about presenting to 40 other people or more.

GULP!!
NEED WATER!!!
HELP!!!

I was so nervous that I thought seriously about going to the airport and flying home. I joined IBM to be a Systems Engineer (technical role) and not to sell. It wasn't what I thought I had signed up for.

Next day, I'm sweating bullets as one by one the others went up, donned the microphone, and delivered their presentation. Going alphabetically gave me plenty of time to sweat before we get to the S's.

It's my time so I go to the front. The instructor helps me with the microphone and I begin my presentation. You may not be aware of this but when your mouth gets really dry, your tongue actually tries to stick to the roof of your mouth as you talk. When it releases it can make a distinct 'pop' sound. Mine was popping on almost every other word and I could hear it distinctly and with the microphone I thought others could as well.

I finally finished the ordeal and went to my seat with what seemed to be the normal applause that everyone else received before me. At any rate, my heart is still ticking and I am so relieved. Ecstatic, actually!

After everyone completed their presentation, we take a break. Many of us were standing around complimenting one another and feeling generally better than when the day began.

*It's at this point that I learned the **most valuable lesson** you can learn about presenting in front of a group of people.*

I complimented one lady who did an exceptional job. In her introduction we learned that she was a former school teacher, someone that is in front of people all the time. Her presentation was very relaxed and well done; everyone thought so. It's at this point she says, "I was scared to death because of all the people with Computer Science, Accounting, and Business degrees. My education is in History and I'm intimidated beyond belief."

That's when I learned that when it comes to public speaking, most of us get nervous, or even scared. We are all very much in the same boat for different reasons.

It will pay you dividends to develop presentation skills. My presentation skills are somewhat advanced since I've used them a lot. I still get nervous even in a small "all hands meeting". It's ok!!

139

Many IT organizations develop a reputation of being poor communicators. The main reason is that they don't really take the initiative to communicate. It takes work to communicate well and it creates opportunity for differences of opinion to surface. It would be so much easier to just 'do the job' and not have to talk to the client or user, right?

Yes, it would.

It wouldn't be very effective or achieve much success though. You see, your success has a lot to do with the perception your client, users, and senior management has on your results and how you go about achieving them. When you don't communicate well, it's very hard for them to perceive the real value you provide.

K. Ability to Track and Measure Performance

Remember the four groups we identified that you need to communicate effectively with? These same groups need to hear and see quantifiable progress. A good manager identifies criteria that should be assessed and tracked to measure performance of the team and individuals.

The better you can quantify performance achievement for your client, senior management, peers, and staff the stronger you'll be able to achieve the results you want. People deal well with specifics; they handle fog and cloudiness poorly.

With each area of IT there is different criteria that should be tracked and measured. In general terms, you want to measure productivity, quality, and return on investment.

Let's look at an example situation by looking at a programming support group. You can apply some of this to most any organization within IT.

You say we need to measure three things in my Support Programming organization:

- productivity
- quality
- return on investment

Where do we begin?

Well, in fact, each issue impacts the other two to an extent. Let's take return on investment first.

Return on Investment

There are a couple of simple measurements that you can do to establish a return on investment. The purists among you will say that my approach here is not really calculating a return on investment and you will be correct. It does equate to the investment that the company is placing in the organization.

Calculate the organization's total cost as a per cent of the company's revenue. You might need to use a smaller part of the company revenue that is appropriate to tying the organization cost being measured to an appropriate revenue source. This establishes a baseline that is important to know. In general, your efforts in the future should be seeing the cost as a per cent of revenue declining if you are improving your organization's productivity and quality. Early on you may see it increase if you have to make some investments due to skill gaps or a lack of sufficient resources to accomplish the things needed by the company.

Cost as % of revenue = total organization cost / revenue

You better know this number if you are the CIO.

Another calculation that you can use to measure return of the investment in your programming organization is to calculate the cost per user for your company by dividing the total organization cost by the number of users. This dollar figure should decline as your company grows.

Avg. IT cost per user = total IT organization cost / number of users

142

For large projects, it may be required to provide a return on investment calculation for the company to justify spending the money. In this area there are plenty of ROI tutorials that can help you understand ROI to any extent that you wish. In general, I have found that senior management wants to know the total cost, the cash flow requirements, and the number of months it takes to pay the company back when the benefits are achieved. I've never been turned down when I've had a reasonable payback timeframe and a solid grasp of these issues.

Payback = total project cost / average monthly benefit savings

Another saying that I have always liked, "If it doesn't positively impact the bottom line, it may not be worth doing." That's not to say there are not worthwhile or essential projects that always fit that criteria, but in general, you always want to do the things that helps you move forward, not backward.

Quality
Measuring quality for a programming support team is easier than you might think. In simplest terms, you can keep a count of how many programming projects are put into production that work and how many have problems. A simple count, to be sure, but it's the start of measuring quality.

Obviously, I would measure much more than that.

To determine measurement criteria for a functional department like programming support, you need to break the process of programming support down into its functional steps. Let's see, in programming support, you program, , and, , , you, , , , ,

OK, OK, I'll help you out, at least from my own perspective.

143

Programming support organizations essentially have 5 functional steps that I believe can be and should be measured. And, they can all be measured easily. These steps are:

1. Design
2. Programming
3. IT (internal) QA
4. User (external) QA
5. Implementation

My belief is that to establish the highest quality, you need to measure each area. A very simple way to do this is to create a spreadsheet like the one below that keeps count of where problems occur for each project that you work on. Over time you should see a trend develop in certain columns that point to your "opportunities" for improvement.

Before we look at it, a bit of explanation is needed.

First, you track and measure things so you can help your staff that might be struggling. Many may know that they are struggling but it helps immensely when you can show the numbers.

Second, it's important that you are clear on responsibilities so that you know who's name is associated with a project in a given functional area. Ultimately you have to get to the individual(s) causing the breakage and you can't do it if the responsibilities are unclear.

Third, let's talk about the functional areas that I listed above:

Design – defining the project, establishing the specific deliverables, and getting client agreement on the project design. Too many projects fail because the work is not properly defined on the front end as to what the programming group must develop.

Programming – includes the actual programming work and the programmer's testing of the work before turning it over to the IT QA focus.

IT QA – Programmers should never be allowed to put program changes into production without another set of eyes testing their work. The IT QA (quality assurance) resource has responsibility to fully test the changes prior to giving it to the user/client for testing.

User QA – The final testing by users of the application prior to putting into production.

Implementation – The process whereby the IT resource puts programming code changes into production.

You can't improve the quality of the programming support organization if you don't know exactly where the problems are occurring and by whom. Keeping a count for each programming project in each of these functional areas will begin quantifying what's going on.

You may also find that once your organization knows you are monitoring and developing a quantitative measurement, the quality will magically improve on it's own.

That's fine; we are after the results. People get things done more effectively when they know someone cares and places importance on it. Let's look at the spreadsheet.

Programming Support - Quality Measurement

6/1/01

Project	Hr.Est.	Design	Program	IT-QA	User QA	Implem.	Total
Project-1							
Project-2							
Project-3							
Project-4							
Project-5							
Project-6							
Project-7							
Project-8							
Project-9							
Project-10							

Can you tell that I believe in keeping it simple? Well, believe it or not, this document and just a little more information will tell a significant amount about the quality of your programming business.

You want to list only the projects that have been assigned and are being worked on or have been completed. By including the column for the estimated hours (Hr.Est.), you will get a sense of problem trends that occur based upon size of projects.

Every time you detect a break in a functional area for a project you add 1 to the block prior to it. For example, if IT-QA finds a problem with the Project1 program given to them from the programmer who programmed it and has to send it back, add 1 to the programmer column in the project's row. Every time IT-QA sends it back to the programmer, add 1 to the number in the programmer row for Project1 until it passes and goes to User QA. If User QA detects a problem, add 1 to the IT-QA column and so on.

Normally, problem notices for Design are discovered at either IT-QA, User QA, or Implementation. It takes a bit of discretion, but you shouldn't fault your programmer for building something that misses the mark because the design is wrong, unless of course he is the resource responsible for design.

As you keep track of the problem issues that occur, a trend should begin to develop. Keeping track at this level lets you determine where the problems are. If you have a dozen programmers, you may want to add a column for the programmer name or keep separate sheets for each programmer so you can determine which resources are effective and which ones need help.

My opinion is that a high quality organization has very few numbers in each column. It is appropriate for the programming column to have higher numbers, but you should be able to tell easily if your programmer is doing a proper level of testing before sending to the QA resource. Posting it for review helps the team reinforce it's own improvement.

An immature organization will have a challenge implementing this scorecard. They will already be struggling to develop change management processes, project management processes, etc. It may take a while before you can trust your staff to keep track of these issues. It can benefit you by doing them yourself in the beginning. It's simple and takes minimal time to get the input during project status meetings.

There are plenty of tools available to help you manage more effectively. Sometimes, a pen and paper is all you need. You'll be surprised at the improvements you can achieve once you understand where the challenge is and begin to coach (help) the resources needing your help.

Productivity
Measuring productivity is the third general area that you want to measure in our programming support example. This part is a bit more difficult to measure because you aren't always using exact numbers but you can get close enough for horseshoes as they say. And in reality, you just need to get within a reasonable range.

In the programming example, I would recommend two measurements to look at productivity. First is the most important and that's the ultimate output of the organization. If you take a look at the project completions that are put into production on a monthly basis, you should be able to quantify the approximate project hours that are getting accomplished each month (boil it down to just programming hours if that helps).

After a few months you should see a trend. There will be some fluctuations because some months will see implementations of rather large projects that were worked on for many months. Still, over the course of 6 months, you can draw a trend line and it will begin to tell you if it's increasing or decreasing.

Improving quality will improve effective output so as your focus on quality shows improvement you are going to start seeing improvements in your productivity.

The second area that I would monitor is in each individual's productivity. You can break a programmer's monthly output into programming hours accomplished for the projects that were completed. Again, there will be fluctuations but a trend line will begin to form in a few months when you plot the total project completion hours every month.

Be sure to only total the number of hours for just those projects that were completed and went into production when you plot the hourly numbers. You're looking for effective output. This is not a perfect way to look at productivity but will be able to give you a good indication.

VIII. <u>Keep a Scorecard</u>

Just as it was important for you to define and communicate your plans, it is also a key part of managing IT resources to keep a scorecard. Take some time with this and develop a measurement system that helps you view your business in a manner that is important for your company. There are many areas of IT that you might consider keeping score on.

Why do we want to keep score?

To improve!!

Keeping statistics or monitoring costs are important elements of understanding your true business in whatever IT position you hold. Understanding the business is essential for improvement and achieving greater success. It also sets you apart from your counterparts.

The true business of any IT manager should be more than simply taking care of the technical part of his operation. The company needs you to understand the dynamics and cause/effect relationships of your business as well.

Every organization can improve just like every individual can improve. Gathering the appropriate data can point you to where you need to focus your attention.

Some scorecards that are important:

- Cost as per cent of revenue
- IT cost per user
- Programming quality
- Infrastructure quality
- Programming productivity
- Infrastructure productivity
- Support desk statistics
    - Call volume
    - Resource productivity
    - Client frequency
    - Reason frequency
    - Time to resolution
- Project completions
- Savings from key projects

Sidebar: *An example of how a scorecard can be helpful might be to show your staff and client the value of implementing certain procedures in a Support Desk. Let's say your Support Desk receives 100 printer calls a month. You take a look at the calls and decide many of them could be avoided if training were provided to a certain department. If you are tracking the calls, it's easy to show the 'before' and 'after' effect of the training.*

Powerful medicine that can by used throughout the IT department. Watch their eyes open!!

IX. <u>Communicate Successes</u>

Communicating your successes is an important item that's often overlooked. You should keep track of successes as well as your failures. Some of the best learning experiences are from our failures. They are the tougher lessons but extremely valuable.

IT managers need to communicate the successes to those 4 groups we identified earlier – senior management, peers, clients, and IT staff. When you get ready to communicate your successes it causes you to reflect on what the team has accomplished in the past "x" months. Every time that I go through this process, I'm surprised. Every single time.

The reason for the surprise is that an IT manager is often dealing with challenges and problems; it's part of the nature of the work, or should I say "beast"?   When you're dealing with problems, never-ending client needs, etc. much of the time, it's hard to think about the good things that are getting done.

Reflecting and going through this exercise of quantifying the organization's achievements will help everyone better appreciate the things that are getting done.

Your staff needs to hear it. Part of the job is to reinforce and motivate.

Your peers will appreciate it because they like to know what's getting done.

Your clients need to know because they can get lost on what they don't have if you let them.

Senior management needs to know. They also like having positive information to share with other parts of the company, clients, and board members.

The bottom line is that everyone will probably be surprised and more appreciative of the IT staff. Part of the job as an IT manager it to provide some rah-rah.

Share your story with enthusiasm and pride; you have worked hard for it to be sure. Your staff will respect you for it and will be motivated by it. Success breeds success. Senior management will appreciate your positive efforts and needs their IT organization to be highly motivated, focused, and effective.

Share the good news.

APPENDIX – IT Assessment
A-1. Senior Management Questionnaire

Name: _____ Position: _____

Dept: _____

1. What is the company (or department) mission or purpose?

2. Is the mission statement written and conveyed to all employees?

3. What is the company (or department) 3 to 5-year plan?

4. What are the company (or department) growth plans/requirements for the next 12-18 months?

5. How does the company (department) plan to achieve it's growth?

6. How does technology fit into the company plans?

7. What are the most important things that IT needs to focus on to support the company (department) business plans (both current and future)?

8. What dependencies does the company (or department) have on technology?

9. What are the company's (or department's) greatest challenges?

10. How well are the technology resources supporting your business needs?

11. What are the IT organization's greatest challenges from your perspective?

APPENDIX – IT Assessment
A-2. Department Manager Questionnaire

Name: _____ **Dept.:** _____
Position: _____

1. What is your department's primary mission/objective?

2. To what extent do you depend upon IT support?

3. What are your department's greatest challenges?

4. What are the IT department's greatest challenges from your perspective?

5. How well does IT meet it's commitments?

6. Describe the responsiveness of the IT organization to your business needs.

7. Do you have upcoming plans that depend upon technology for success?

8. Describe your department's relationship with the IT organization.

A-3. Client Questionnaire

Name: _____   Client: _____

1. How long have you been a client of _____?

2. Why did you buy their products or services?

3. Would you buy them again?   Explain.

4. Tell me about your business.

5. How are priorities established with _____?

6. How responsive is _____ to your business needs?

7. What are your greatest challenges as it relates to
    _____?

8. Do you have future plans that _____ should be
    anticipating?

9. Does _____ understand your challenges, priorities,
    etc.?

10. What are your recommendations to improve your relationship
    with _____?

APPENDIX – IT Assessment
A-4. IT Resource Questionnaire

Name: _____ Position: _____

1. How long have you been with the company?

2. What did you do before joining the company?

3. Describe your current responsibilities.

4. What do you like about your current position?

5. What do you not like about your current position?

6. How would you describe your department's mission?

7. How well do you believe the department is meeting it's objectives?

8. What are the major challenges for your department?

9. What do you see as the company's key challenges?

10. Who is your client and tell me about them?

11. What do you want to be when you grow up?

12. What are the top 3 things you'd like to see improved or changed?

13. When was your last review and salary increase?

14. How does management measure your performance?

APPENDIX
B. Issues Priority Matrix

Pri.	Task	Est. $$	Lead time	Prereq.	Dependencies
1					
2					
3					
4					
5					
6					
7					
8					
9					
10					
11					
12					
13					
14					
15					
16					
17					
18					
19					
20					

APPENDIX
C. IT Project Hierarchy

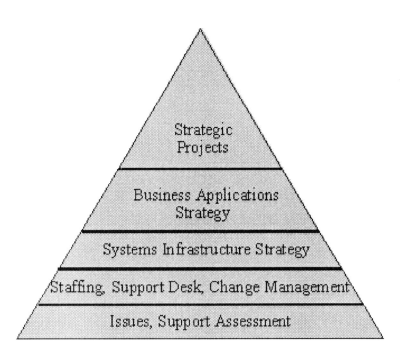

Strategic Projects

Business Applications Strategy

Systems Infrastructure Strategy

Staffing, Support Desk, Change Management

Issues, Support Assessment

APPENDIX
D-1. Change Request – Programming

Information Technology
Programming Request No. _____

Requested By: _____ Dept. _____

Request Date: _____ Priority Request _____ (High, Med, Low)

Supervisor Approval: _____ Date: _____

Description of Problem / Issue: (Attach supporting documentation as needed)

_____

_____

_____

_____

_____

_____

_____

Justification:

Savings / Benefits (Be specific as possible): _____

_____

_____

_____

IT Department Use Only

Est. Programming hours _____ Comments : _____
Est. Benefit $ value _____ _____
Est. Programming cost _____ _____
_____
_____

Employee Equipment Change request

_____ Add   Requested by: _____
_____ Change   Request Date: _____
_____ Delete

Employee Name: _____
Department: _____
Effective Date: _____
Physical Location: _____
                   _____

Equipment Needed:

_____ PC
_____ Laptop Computer
_____ New Phone
      Special phone needs ?
_____
_____
_____ Fax
_____ External modem line

Software Needs:

_____ MS/Office (Included w/PC)
_____ FRX
Other software needs:
      _____
      _____
      _____

Services Needed:

_____ AS/400 (Billing,A/R)
_____ CA
_____ NC,SC
_____ New Jersey
_____ Indiana
_____ Ohio
_____ Texas
      AS/400 Infinium (Acct.)
_____ FRX

Primary Printer _____

Other services needed:
      _____
      _____
      _____

Submit form to Information Technology Support Desk for completion:

APPENDIX
D-3. Programming Backlog Request Log

				Expected		Est.	
5/6/02	PROJECT	PRI	Req. By	Start	End	Prog. Hours	Status / Comments
1							
2							
3							
4							
5							
6							
7							
8							
9							
10							
11							
12							
13							
14							
15							
16							
17							
18							
19							
20							

Programming Backlog - Active Requests

APPENDIX
E. New Employee Orientation

A. Quick tour and introductions
B. The Company
C. Mission
D. The company's business
E. Organization
F. Key departments relative to IT support
G. Strategic plans
H. Clients
- Their needs for IT services
- Key clients
- The best and the worst, , ,and why
- Key needs
- Plans
I. Company Departments
- Key departments and their key people
- Department needs
- Plans
J. Benefits Orientation and paperwork with Human
Resources
- Medical/dental insurance
- Life insurance
- 401k
- W4
- Vacation/holiday/sick day policy
- Employee Handbook
- Confidentiality agreement
- Non-solicitation agreement

E. New Employee Orientation (continued)

K. IT Organization
- Mission
- Organization chart and major focus areas
- Job description and responsibilities of the new hire
- Role within the IT organization
- Key focus areas of the new position
- Keys to success
- Overview of other key IT staff and their responsibilities
- Challenges
- Opportunities

L. IT Vision and plan for the future

M. Key projects and status

N. IT Procedures/Processes that affect the new employee

O. Performance planning and performance review guidelines

P. Career planning approach and guidelines

Q. Training guidelines

R. Miscellaneous
- Phone list
- After hours IT phone list
- Expense reporting
- Timesheets (if required)
- Security codes, cards, etc.
- User-ID & passwords to systems

APPENDIX
E. New Employee Orientation (continued)

In addition to the orientation, don't forget to coordinate the preparation of certain things such as:

A. Identify cube/office location
B. Phone setup
C. PC/workstation setup
D. Printer configuration setup
E. USER-ID and password setup
F. Office supplies
G. Building, facility, parking access cards
H. Business card order